WOMAN'S DAY®

The Only 25 Recipes You'll Ever Need

WOMAN'S DAY®:

The Only 25 Recipes You'll Ever Need

SIDNEY BURSTEIN

Illustrated by Celia Mitchell

DOUBLEDAY
New York London Toronto Sydney Auckland

PUBLISHED BY DOUBLEDAY
a division of Bantam Doubleday Dell Publishing Group, Inc.
666 Fifth Avenue, New York, New York 10103

DOUBLEDAY and the portrayal of an anchor
with a dolphin are trademarks of Doubleday,
a division of Bantam Doubleday Dell Publishing Group, Inc.

"Woman's Day" is a registered trademark
of Diamandis Communications, Inc.

Library of Congress Cataloging-in-Publication Data

Woman's day: the only 25 recipes you'll ever need / by Sidney Burstein. — 1st ed.
     p.   cm.
   1. Cookery.   I. Burstein, Sidney.   II. Woman's day.
  TX714.W647   1990   89-48669
641.5 — dc20   CIP

ISBN 0-385-41179-0

*This book
is dedicated to
Ray
and to my father,
Louie.*

ACKNOWLEDGMENTS

I would like to thank the following people:

Ellen Levine for thinking of me.

Elizabeth Alston for guidance.

Lucy Emerson Sullivan for her initial spark that lit the fires and kept them burning to fuel this, my first book.

Miriam Rubin for reading and editing the manuscript.

Jill Wellenbach for her critical observations.

The Game Night crew: Trudy, Fran, and Larry, who ate everything, rarely complained, and occasionally raved. And even Marjorie, who loved the Sacher Brownies, then called three days later to say they were too sweet.

FOREWORD

Some truths I know now that I wish I'd known as a young wife: Life in the kitchen is only as complicated as you want it to be. And you don't have to approach a recipe as if it were a diagram for brain surgery in order to please your family and dinner guests.

When I was a new bride, I cooked as if I were performing a chemistry experiment—one that would blow up the entire house should I err and add a pinch too much salt. Fortunately for my nerves, I gradually allowed myself to relax around the kitchen. And I learned that most recipes aren't strict formulas but are guides to creating dishes that welcome some experimentation. My own joy of cooking really began when it dawned on me that the basic cream sauce I'd labored over could be turned into a totally different kind of sauce just by adding a few new ingredients! After I mastered that concept, cooking was fun.

Another major truth about cooking occurred to me after I'd become editor in chief of Woman's Day. As I reviewed the hundreds of recipes our Food Department produces in the course of a year, I realized that most were variations on a few basic themes—just like my experience with the "magic" cream sauce. It was that idea that led to this book.

What you're holding in your hand right now is more than just a collection of twenty-five recipes. This book is really the foundation you need to become an expert in the kitchen. Because every recipe includes three variations, you can go from simple to complex dishes without becoming confused by unfamiliar cooking terms and techniques. That in itself can save you time—and what woman (or man, for that matter) doesn't want to save time these days?

If you already know your way around the kitchen, I hope this book becomes one of your basic reference cookbooks. And if you're a newly married woman or man who's wondering what comes after learning to boil water, lucky you! You're about to embark on a great adventure.

Ellen Levine

Editor-in-Chief
Woman's Day

CONTENTS

FIRST COURSES

SALADS/SIDE DISHES

4 **Broiled Tomato**   Broiled Tomato with Rosemary / Tomato Provençale / Tex-Mex Stuffed Tomato   **8**

5 **Mashed Potatoes**   Mashed Potato Soufflé / Mashed Potato Croquettes / Quick Chilled Soup (Vichyssoise)   **10**

6 **Rice Pilaf**   Middle Eastern Pilau / Spanish Rice / Cold Rice Salad   **12**

7 **Salade Niçoise**   Antipasto / Pan Bagnat (Niçoise Hero) / Pasta Salad Provençale   **14**

8 **Steamed Fresh Vegetables**   Vegetables à la Russe / Au Gratin Vegetables / Stir-fry   **16**

SAUCES

9 **Fresh Tomato Sauce**   Chunky Tomato Salad / Gazpacho Soup / Salsa   **18**

10 **White Sauce/Béchamel**   Cheese Sauce / Herb Sauce / Chicken Gravy   **20**

11 **Salad Dressing**   Oriental Sesame Dressing / Green Herb Dressing / Roquefort or Goat Cheese Dressing   **22**

MAIN COURSES

DESSERTS

AUTHOR'S INTRODUCTION

This is a cookbook, a how-to book, a guide. It is a simple primer. It invites you to learn new techniques, practice them, then try a variation or two. With a few simple twists, the twenty-five recipes will yield a hundred dishes featuring short ingredient lists and minimal preparation time.

Use this book often. It should have coffee stains and bits of biscuit dough stuck to the pages, handwritten comments on what needs a pinch more salt and what was exceptionally yummy.

Each of the twenty-five recipes is on a left-hand page. On the right-hand page you will find three variations followed by relevant tips.

Cross-references to the twenty-five basic recipes in this book are capitalized. Cross-references to the variations appear in upper- and lowercase. New ingredients or amounts in the variations are listed in italic. Asterisks refer to the tips that follow the variations.

Recipes include Soups, Salads, Side Dishes, Main Courses, and Desserts, and I suggest how to match the various courses to create fun menus. These meals are simple enough to prepare for a week-night dinner but special enough for company. The ROAST CHICKEN is especially simple. It has only one main ingredient. (You guessed it!)

The recipes call for fresh, readily available ingredients but occasionally recommend convenient alternatives when items are out of season or when you are in a hurry. All the recipes make use of the basic kitchen equipment outlined in How to Stock a Kitchen (page 70).

Simplicity and good taste are the foundation of this book but so are proper nutrition and a balance of ingredients. I am keeping a watchful eye on sodium, cholesterol, sugar, and fat.

There is no magic here except perhaps the rabbit you pull out of a hat at the kitchen table as dinner is about to be served.

Sidney

 **READ ME FIRST**

This little glossary will explain ingredients and techniques found in the book. *Read it at once.*

BAY LEAF Always remove a bay leaf before serving a recipe. The leaf is quite sharp.

BLACK PEPPER, FRESHLY GROUND Buy a small pepper mill. Fill it with whole black peppercorns (available in supermarket spice racks). Keep it in the kitchen or on the dining room table (if you have one).

When a recipe calls for "freshly ground black pepper," grab the pepper mill and give it two or three good grinds or turns to release the ground pepper. On many pepper mills, you can adjust the grind (by loosening or tightening a screw) from coarse to fine, depending on your preference. A coarser grind will add texture, crunch, and more of an immediate "kick" than a fine powder.

Cracked black pepper is a very coarse grind found in supermarket spice racks. Or, use your pepper mill to produce coarse ground pepper.

BREAD CRUMBS Use plain (unflavored) store-bought crumbs. Or, save stale bread. Grate it or make crumbs in a blender or food processor.

BUTTER Butter is always sweet, unsalted.

CHICKEN BROTH Chicken broth is a very basic and important ingredient. A good flavorful broth is the foundation of an assortment of recipes in this book.

Freeze any leftover strained CHICKEN SOUP in one-cup containers to use whenever chicken broth is called for.

Quality broth is available in cans in the supermarket. (College Inn and Swanson's are good examples.) If you have found a dehydrated chicken broth cube or packet that you enjoy, use it.

CILANTRO/CORIANDER Cilantro, also called fresh coriander and Chinese parsley, is a pungent and aromatic herb sold in many ethnic (Latin, Oriental, Spanish, Portuguese) markets. Substitute parsley if coriander is unavailable, but it lacks the flavor and punch. Dried cilantro is sometimes available on supermarket spice racks. Use about ½ teaspoon for each tablespoon of fresh called for. However, it too lacks the flavor and punch.

CORN If it's summer and the corn is high, substitute fresh corn for canned corn. Four ears will yield about 2 cups of cut kernels. Remove husks and silk from the corn. Using a paring knife, cut down the length of each ear to release the kernels. A 16-ounce can, drained, and one 10-ounce package of frozen will each yield 2 cups of corn kernels.

EGGS Eggs are always large.

FLOUR Flour is always unbleached white all-purpose.

To measure flour, spoon the flour lightly into a measuring cup until overflowing. Level off the top with a knife or spatula. Do not scoop the flour with the measuring cup. (You will pack it in and have an inaccurate measure.)

GARLIC, MINCED Generally, the recipes call for "garlic cloves, minced." This refers to cloves of garlic from a standard-size head usually containing about twenty to twenty-five skin-wrapped cloves of varying sizes. Use your judgment. If you love garlic, use a larger clove; or use two.

The easiest way to peel a clove of garlic is to place it on a cutting board. Holding a chef's knife, give the garlic a whack with the side of the blade to crush it slightly. The skin will break and can easily be peeled.

Chop it fine or use a garlic press.

GINGER, MINCED FRESH To mince fresh ginger, peel the thin brown skin off a 2-inch piece. Slice it ¼ inch thick and finely chop with a chef's knife, or grate the peeled ginger (without slicing) on a grater. If you absolutely love ginger, buy a ginger grater.

HALVE A RECIPE Several variations ask you to "make half a recipe." This means cutting each ingredient of the recipe in half. For example, 2¼ cups flour, halved, would yield 1⅛ cups or 1 cup plus 2 tablespoons; 1 tablespoon sugar, halved, is 1½ teaspoons.

The recipe is prepared in the same manner.

LEMON, GRATED RIND OF A The rind of a lemon is the outermost yellow layer of skin, also called the "zest." Rinse or wipe a whole lemon. Hold the lemon in one hand. Using the fine side (smallest holes) of a grater, grate just the rind and not the bitter white pith underneath. This will yield a small clump of finely shredded rind. (It may cling to the grater; scrape it off and use it.)

LEMON JUICE or LIME JUICE It is preferable to buy fresh lemons and limes and squeeze your own juice. Otherwise, use bottled unsweetened juice.

MICROWAVE All microwave recipes were cooked in a full-power carousel microwave (650 to 700 watts) using microwave-safe containers and plastic wrap. Recipes were cooked on HIGH (full power). If your microwave is less powerful, an adjustment in cooking time must be made. If your microwave does not have a carousel, you may have to rotate the dish while cooking. See the manufacturer's instructions.

OIL When a recipe calls for oil, use the oil of your choice. An ordinary vegetable or "light" olive oil is fine.

OLIVE OIL Olive oils are nearly as varied and complex as wines. Some are very bland, light in color, and lacking in flavor and intensity. Others are dark, robust, and strong in taste. When first buying olive oil, try different brands in small bottles until you find the most appealing flavor.

When sautéing in olive oil, a very strong oil will add its own flavor to the dish. It is your choice.

OVEN, TO HEAT THE Always heat the oven to the correct temperature at least fifteen to twenty minutes before baking is to begin. (You may have a light or other indicator that lets you know when the temperature is reached.) All temperatures are Fahrenheit.

PARMESAN CHEESE The freshest and most flavorful grated cheese is grated at the last moment at home using a small wedge of Parmigiano Reggiano and a hand grater. You can regulate the texture from fine to coarse.

You can also "shave" the wedge using a vegetable peeler. Sprinkle the shavings on a green salad, over pasta, or in a soup.

Freshly grated Parmesan cheese sold loose (by the pound) in cheese shops is excellent. Otherwise, bottled grated cheese is a fair substitute.

RICE There are different types of white rice: long grain, short grain, medium grain, and parboiled or converted. There are aromatic rices: basmati, wehani, Texmati. Each has its own texture and flavor. Experiment with different types. Each will work in these recipes.

Follow the package instructions for cooking times and amounts of liquid.

Precooked five-minute rice will not work in these recipes.

SHALLOT Shallot is a member of the onion family. It is a small bulb (resembling a baby onion but with a slightly reddish skin) with several cloves attached to one root, like garlic. It has a sweet and mild flavor when cooked.

SUGAR Sugar is always white granulated unless otherwise noted.

VANILLA EXTRACT Vanilla extract is pure.

VINEGAR Vinegars are as varied as oils. Flavored ones (herb, fruit, spice, balsamic, rice, cider, wine) add another dimension to the taste; again, your palate will determine which to use.

1 Corn Chowder

4 slices raw bacon, cut into
½-inch pieces

½ cup chopped onion

½ cup diced red bell pepper*
or celery

1 bay leaf

½ teaspoon dried thyme leaves

¼ teaspoon celery salt

1 16-ounce can corn kernels,
drained, about 2 cups

1 16-ounce can cream-style corn

2¼ cups milk

½ to ¾ teaspoon salt

Freshly ground black pepper

MAKES 6 CUPS

"Chowder" derives from the French chaudière, *a cauldron or kettle in which great fish soups were cooked.*

1   In a soup pot, cook the bacon 5 to 7 minutes, until crisp. Spoon off and discard all but about 1 tablespoon fat.

2   Stir in the onion, bell pepper, bay leaf, thyme, and celery salt. Cook, stirring, 8 to 10 minutes, until soft.

3   Stir in the corn and milk. Cover and simmer 20 minutes. Season with the salt and pepper. Remove the bay leaf; serve.

Tip   *To dice a bell pepper, place the pepper on its side on a cutting board; trim ½ inch off the stem end. Cut the pepper lengthwise in quarters. Trim any white membranes. Using a chef's knife, cut each piece into ½-inch squares.*

Variation 1 *P*ENNSYLVANIA DUTCH CORN AND NOODLE SOUP   MAKES 4 TO 5 CUPS

This is flavored with bacon and thickened ever so slightly with the starch from the noodles cooking in the broth.

Make CORN CHOWDER with the following changes: In a large soup pot, cook the bacon, onion, bell pepper, bay leaf, thyme, and celery salt as above. Stir in the corn kernels and *4 cups chicken broth*. Omit the cream-style corn and milk. Heat to a boil. Stir in *2 ounces wide egg noodles*. Lower the heat and simmer, uncovered, just until the noodles are tender. Remove the bay leaf. Season with salt and pepper to taste. Serve sprinkled with *chopped chives*.

Variation 2 *S*POON BREAD   SERVES 6 AS A SIDE DISH

A corn pudding, this is not a "bread" at all but is more like a corn soufflé without the beaten egg whites.

Make CORN CHOWDER with the following changes: Heat the oven to 375°. Omit the bay leaf and cream-style corn. Heat the mixture just to a simmer. Slowly whisk in *¾ cup yellow cornmeal*. Cook, stirring, 2 to 3 minutes, until very thick. Cool slightly. Stir in *3 eggs, lightly beaten, and 1 teaspoon baking powder,* until smooth. Bake in a *buttered* 6-cup soufflé dish for 30 minutes. Lower the heat to 350°. Bake 15 minutes, until puffed and golden. Serve immediately.

Variation 3 *S*KILLET CORN BREAD   12 SERVINGS

Make CORN CHOWDER with the following changes: Heat the oven to 400°. In a 12-inch oven-proof or cast-iron skillet, cook the bacon as above. Add the onion, bell pepper, thyme, and celery salt. Omit the bay leaf. Sauté, stirring, 8 to 10 minutes. In a bowl, stir the cream-style corn, *3 eggs, only ¼ cup milk, and 2 tablespoons oil,* until smooth. Omit the corn kernels. In a second bowl, toss *2 cups yellow cornmeal, 1 tablespoon baking powder, 1 tablespoon sugar,* ½ teaspoon salt, and freshly ground black pepper. Stir the dry ingredients and sautéed vegetables into the corn and egg mixture. Heat *1 tablespoon oil* in the same skillet over medium heat. Pour in the batter. Cook 1 minute. Transfer to the oven and bake 15 minutes, until firm to the touch. Loosen the edge with a knife. Cool slightly. Cut into 12 wedges and serve from the skillet.

2 Chicken Soup

1 chicken, about 3½ pounds, quartered

1 carrot, cut into 2-inch pieces *

1 celery stalk, cut into 2-inch pieces

1 parsnip, peeled and halved

1 turnip, halved

1 medium onion, halved

½ cup parsley sprigs

2 or 3 sprigs fresh dill

2 cloves garlic

9 cups water

½ teaspoon salt, plus additional, to taste

Freshly ground black pepper

MAKES 7 CUPS

Is this the pinnacle of comfort food? For me the aroma alone is a one-way ticket to my mother's kitchen on the eve of a holiday. The soup is gently simmering in a large enamel pot (with a funny lid) planted firmly on a back burner.

1. Place all the ingredients in a large pot.
2. Heat to a boil. Lower heat and simmer uncovered 1¼ hours, skimming the surface as scum rises. Strain the soup. Skim the fat.
3. Reheat and serve.

Tip   *Many supermarket produce shelves stock a packaged fresh vegetable assortment for soup. It usually contains a stalk of celery, an onion, a carrot, a turnip or parsnip, and parsley or dill.*

4

Variation 1 *A*VGOLEMONO

This Greek lemon and dill soup cooks quickly and efficiently in the microwave. There is no avgo *(egg) in this version.*

Make CHICKEN SOUP with the following changes: Set aside 2 cups of strained soup for another use. In a 2½-quart covered microwave-safe casserole, stir *5 cups CHICKEN SOUP, ¼ cup raw rice, ¼ cup chopped fresh dill, and 3 tablespoons fresh lemon juice.* Cover and microwave on HIGH 25 minutes. Season with *salt and freshly ground black pepper.* Sprinkle with *additional chopped fresh dill.* Serve.

Variation 2 *S*TRACCIATELLA

Make CHICKEN SOUP with the following changes: Set aside 3 cups of strained soup for another use. In a soup pot, heat *4 cups CHICKEN SOUP* to a simmer. Stir in *8 cups loosely packed cleaned and trimmed fresh spinach leaves, with stems removed, cut into strips.* Cook 2 minutes to wilt spinach. In a small bowl, stir *yolks of 3 eggs, 2 tablespoons fresh lemon juice, and ⅓ cup freshly grated Parmesan cheese.* Lower the heat under the soup pot and whisk in the yolk mixture. Cook 1 minute, until slightly thickened. Season with salt and freshly ground pepper. Serve with *additional grated Parmesan cheese.*

Variation 3 *T*ORTILLA SOUP

Make CHICKEN SOUP with the following changes: Set aside 3 cups of strained soup for another use. Cut *4 corn tortillas* into ¼-inch strips. Heat the oven to 425° and crisp strips on a baking sheet 10 minutes. In a soup pot, heat *4 cups CHICKEN SOUP* over low heat. Stir in *½ cup corn kernels; 1 ripe but firm small avocado, peeled and cut into 1-inch pieces; 2 tablespoons chopped cilantro; juice of 1 lime; ½ teaspoon ground cumin; and freshly ground black pepper.* Season with *salt.* Cook just until heated through. Sprinkle tortilla strips in each of 4 soup bowls. Ladle in soup. Serve immediately.

Tips   * *To make any of the variations, substitute canned chicken broth for the CHICKEN SOUP if fresh is not available.*

   * *Avgolemono can be cooked, covered, on top of the stove for the same time, until rice is tender. If using ordinary white rice (not converted or parboiled), the soup will thicken as it stands.*

3 *G*arlic Bread

1 loaf bread (about 12 inches long), French, Italian, white, whole wheat, sourdough, or semolina.

¼ cup olive oil

3 or 4 cloves garlic, minced

¼ teaspoon dried oregano leaves

Freshly ground black pepper

2 tablespoons grated Parmesan cheese

SERVES 4 TO 6

Garlic bread is an appetizer, an hors d' oeuvre, a table bread, and something to throw together at midnight for a quick snack.

1 Heat oven to 375°.

2 Halve the bread lengthwise.

3 In a small bowl, stir the oil, garlic, oregano, and pepper. Brush or drizzle oil on each half of the bread.

4 Wrap each half in foil, leaving the tops uncovered. Sprinkle with cheese.

5 Bake 25 minutes, until golden and crusted. With a serrated knife, cut each half into 6 pieces.

Variation 1   CROSTINI

SERVES 6

This is an open-faced, baked and bubbling cheese and garlic toast. It is more filling than GARLIC BREAD.

Make GARLIC BREAD with the following changes: Before baking, top *each* half of the bread with ¼ *pound overlapping slices of mozzarella cheese and 6 anchovies*, crisscrossed. Bake and serve as above.

Variation 2   BRUSCHETTA

SERVES 6

The freshest and ripest tomatoes, chopped, are spooned over baked GARLIC BREAD. The bread absorbs some of the juices. Serve on small plates as a first course.

Make GARLIC BREAD with the following changes: Bake the bread and slice as above. Prepare Chunky Tomato Salad. On a large platter, arrange the bread in one layer, cut side up. Spoon the salad over the bread. Let stand 15 minutes to let the salad juices soak into the bread. Serve as a first course or as part of a summer buffet.

Variation 3   BREAD SALAD

SERVES 4 TO 6 AS A SIDE SALAD

Make GARLIC BREAD with the following changes: Halve the recipe. Omit *cheese*. Do not bake. Cut *the seasoned unbaked loaf* into 1-inch chunks. In a large bowl, toss the bread, *2 large (10 ounces each) ripe tomatoes, cut into 1-inch chunks; ½ medium red onion, thinly sliced; 1 red bell pepper, thinly sliced; ½ cup coarsely chopped fresh parsley and/or fresh basil; ¼ teaspoon salt, and freshly ground black pepper* with ⅓ cup *SALAD DRESSING*. Cover with a plate to weight the salad. Let it stand 1 to 2 hours, tossing occasionally.

4 Broiled Tomato

When tomatoes are full, ripe, and abundant, make any of these simple side dishes. Serve as a brunch vegetable to go with omelets or scrambled eggs. At dinner, serve with steak, chicken, or fish.

1 large ripe but firm tomato, about 8 to 10 ounces

Olive oil

¼ teaspoon light brown sugar

Salt and freshly ground black pepper

SERVES 2

1 Halve the tomato crosswise.

2 Brush the cut side of each half lightly with oil.

3 Sprinkle each half with sugar, salt to taste, and freshly ground black pepper.

4 Place on a small baking sheet. Broil 5 to 7 minutes, until soft to the touch and golden on top. Serve immediately.

Variation 1 BROILED TOMATO WITH ROSEMARY

SERVES 2

Make BROILED TOMATO with the following changes: Omit the sugar. Sprinkle the tops with *1 tablespoon chopped fresh rosemary leaves, or ½ teaspoon dried rosemary* before broiling.

Variation 2 TOMATO PROVENÇALE

SERVES 2

A classic French side dish, the tomato is stuffed with a garlic and crumb mixture.

Make BROILED TOMATO with the following changes: Omit the sugar. Heat the oven to 450°. With a melon baller or spoon, scoop out and discard ½ inch of pulp from each tomato half. In a small bowl, toss *3 tablespoons plain bread crumbs; 1 tablespoon grated Parmesan cheese; 1 tablespoon olive oil; 1 clove garlic, minced; ⅛ teaspoon salt; and freshly ground black pepper.* Stuff the tomato halves with the crumb mixture. Bake 15 minutes, until golden.

Variation 3 TEX-MEX STUFFED TOMATO

SERVES 2

Serve with Beef Fajitas, Chicken Fajitas, or with Stuffed Cajun Sole.

Make BROILED TOMATO with the following changes: Omit the sugar and olive oil. Heat the oven to 450°. With a melon baller or spoon, scoop out and discard the pulp from each tomato half, leaving a ¼-inch shell. In a small bowl, toss *¼ cup corn kernels, ¼ cup diced peeled firm ripe avocado, ¼ cup shredded sharp Cheddar cheese, 1 tablespoon chopped scallion, 1 tablespoon chopped cilantro, 1 tablespoon plain bread crumbs, ⅛ teaspoon salt, and freshly ground black pepper.* Stuff the tomato halves with this mixture, mounding it slightly. Place in a small baking dish. Bake 15 minutes, until golden.

5 **M**ashed Potatoes

The question "Are they real?" is often asked about various things—diamonds, pearls, etc. But in restaurants I inquire about only one item—mashed potatoes.

2 pounds all-purpose potatoes, peeled,* cut into 1½-inch chunks

⅓ cup warm milk

5 tablespoons butter

½ to ¾ teaspoon salt

Freshly ground black pepper

MAKES 4 TO 5 CUPS

1 Cook the potatoes in a pot of lightly salted boiling water about 30 minutes, until easily pierced with a fork. Drain in a colander.

2 Return to the pot or a large bowl. Using a hand mixer, potato masher, or wooden spoon, beat in the milk and butter, until smooth or lumpy, depending on your taste.

3 Season with salt and pepper. Serve.

10

Variation 1 MASHED POTATO SOUFFLÉ

SERVES 6

Make MASHED POTATOES with the following changes: Heat the oven to 425°. Make MASHED POTATOES. Beat in *4 eggs* and *¼ cup grated Parmesan cheese*. Scrape the mixture into a buttered, shallow 1½-quart casserole. Sprinkle with *2 tablespoons plain bread crumbs*. Bake 30 to 40 minutes, until puffed and browned.

Variation 2 MASHED POTATO CROQUETTES

SERVES 4

Make MASHED POTATOES with the following changes: Halve the recipe, or use 2 cups leftover MASHED POTATOES. Shape *2 cups MASHED POTATOES* into 4 patties. In a shallow bowl, whisk *1 egg* and *1 tablespoon water*. In a second bowl, place *a scant (slightly less than) ½ cup plain bread crumbs*. Coat each patty in egg and then in crumbs. Heat *1 tablespoon each butter and oil* in a large nonstick skillet. Fry the patties over medium heat about 5 to 6 minutes, turning several times, until golden and crusted.

Variation 3 QUICK CHILLED SOUP (VICHYSSOISE)

MAKES ABOUT 5 CUPS; SERVES 4 TO 6

Make MASHED POTATOES with the following changes: Halve the recipe, or use 2 cups leftover MASHED POTATOES. In a medium soup pot, whisk *2 cups MASHED POTATOES*, about *3¼ cups chicken broth (two 13¾-ounce cans)*, *⅓ cup chopped scallions,* and *freshly ground black pepper*. Heat to a boil; lower the heat, cover, and simmer 15 minutes, stirring several times. Puree in a food processor or blender, in batches, until smooth; strain the soup if skins were left on the potatoes. Refrigerate 2 hours, until cold. Whisk in *½ cup plain yogurt, sour cream, or heavy cream*, if desired. Serve sprinkled with *chopped scallions*.

Tip   * *If you prefer, and for added fiber, leave the skins on the potatoes.*

11

6 Rice Pilaf

Pilaf, pilaff, pilav, pullao, pilaw, and pilau are Middle Eastern, Persian, North African, or Indian versions of cooked and flavored rice. I call for chicken broth as the cooking liquid to add more flavor; any seasoned and flavorful broth (vegetable or beef) will do.

2 tablespoons olive oil or butter

½ cup chopped onion

½ teaspoon dried thyme leaves

1 bay leaf

1 cup raw white rice*

2 cups chicken broth

Fresh parsley, chopped

MAKES 3 CUPS

1   In a 2-quart saucepan, heat the olive oil or butter over medium heat. Sauté the onion, thyme, and bay leaf 5 minutes.

2   Stir in the rice. Cook 1 to 2 minutes, just until the rice is translucent and coated in oil.

3   Stir in the broth. Heat just to a boil. Cover, lower heat, and simmer 20 minutes, until the liquid is absorbed.

4   Let stand, covered, off the heat, 5 minutes. Remove the bay leaf. Fluff with a fork, sprinkle with chopped parsley, and serve.

Variation 1 MIDDLE EASTERN PILAU

MAKES 3 CUPS

Make RICE PILAF with the following changes: Omit the thyme. After adding the rice to the onion, stir in ¼ cup shelled pistachios, ¼ cup raisins or dried currants, ¼ cup chopped fresh parsley, and ½ teaspoon ground cinnamon. Stir in the broth. Cook as above; omit the additional parsley.

Variation 2 SPANISH RICE

MAKES 3 CUPS

Make RICE PILAF with the following changes: Sauté ½ cup chopped red bell pepper with the onion and bay leaf. Use dried oregano instead of thyme. Add ¼ teaspoon saffron threads to the onion with the rice. Stir in the broth and cook as above. Sprinkle with 1 tablespoon drained capers instead of parsley before serving.

Variation 3 COLD RICE SALAD

MAKES 3 CUPS

Serve as a side dish or as part of a buffet.

Make RICE PILAF with the following changes: Cool cooked RICE PILAF to room temperature. In a large bowl, toss the rice with ½ cup pitted and slivered imported black olives, ¼ cup sliced scallions, 2 tablespoons olive oil, and 1 tablespoon slivered orange peel.*

Tips * For rice, see Glossary (page xiii), Ingredient Substitutions (page 65), and Secrets of a Competent Cook (page 68).

* To cut "slivered orange peel," using a vegetable peeler, cut off 2- to 3-inch strips of peel (orange part only). With a sharp chef's knife, cut strips crosswise into slivers.

7 $alade Niçoise

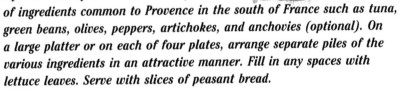

½ pound green beans, ends trimmed

½ pound small potatoes, unpeeled, cut into 1-inch chunks

1 cup canned chick-peas, drained

1 14- or 16-ounce can artichoke hearts, drained

1 6- or 8-ounce jar roasted peppers, drained; or 2 small red bell peppers, roasted*

4 plum tomatoes, quartered

1 small red onion, sliced

1 cup pitted imported black olives

1 6-ounce can tuna, drained

2 eggs, hard-cooked and quartered

4 to 6 anchovies (optional)

1 cup SALAD DRESSING

SERVES 4

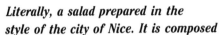

Literally, a salad prepared in the style of the city of Nice. It is composed of ingredients common to Provence in the south of France such as tuna, green beans, olives, peppers, artichokes, and anchovies (optional). On a large platter or on each of four plates, arrange separate piles of the various ingredients in an attractive manner. Fill in any spaces with lettuce leaves. Serve with slices of peasant bread.

1 Cook the beans in a pot of boiling salted water 4 to 5 minutes, until cooked and crisp. Rinse under cold water; drain.

2 Place the potatoes in a sauce pan of cold water. Heat to a boil. Simmer 10 to 12 minutes, until tender. Rinse; drain.

3 On a large platter, arrange separate piles of all ingredients; crisscross the anchovies over the quartered eggs.

4 Serve the dressing on the side.

Variation 1 *A*NTIPASTO

Prepare SALADE NIÇOISE with the following changes: Omit the potatoes, eggs, and tuna. Substitute *3 ounces thin-sliced Genoa salami and 3 ounces cubed or sliced provolone cheese.* Arrange as above with anchovies on the side. Serve with bread sticks or Italian bread, oil and vinegar, or SALAD DRESSING.

Variation 2 *P*AN BAGNAT (NIÇOISE HERO)

THIS ENORMOUS SANDWICH SERVES 4

Make SALADE NIÇOISE with the following changes: Omit the potatoes and eggs. Halve a large (12-inch round) *peasant bread* horizontally. Scoop out half the bread from each piece. Brush the inside of each half with *2 tablespoons SALAD DRESSING,* or drizzle with *oil and vinegar.* Fill the bottom half with the following as listed: *4 ounces cooked green beans, ½ cup chick-peas*, the artichoke hearts, roasted peppers, tomatoes, onion, ½ cup pitted olives, flaked tuna, and anchovies. Drizzle on 2 tablespoons SALAD DRESSING. Cover with the top half of the bread. Press down lightly, cut into quarters and serve.

Variation 3 *P*ASTA SALAD PROVENÇALE

SERVES 4

Make SALADE NIÇOISE with the following changes: Omit the potatoes and 1 egg. Cook *8 ounces macaroni, ziti, or penne* according to package instructions. Rinse and drain. In a large bowl toss the pasta; green beans; chick-peas; halved artichoke hearts; roasted peppers, cut into 1-inch chunks; tomatoes, cut into 1-inch chunks; red onion, chopped; pitted olives; and flaked tuna. Mince the anchovies and stir into ⅔ cup *SALAD DRESSING.* Toss the salad with the dressing. Season with *salt and freshly ground black pepper.* Sieve* or grate 1 hard-cooked egg on top as garnish.

Tips   * *To roast bell peppers char the whole peppers, carefuly turning them over a gas burner using metal tongs; or place them on a baking sheet under the broiler, turning occasionally until blackened. Transfer to a paper bag. Close the bag and let "steam" 15 minutes. Peel and discard the blackened skin. Remove the stems and seeds.*

* *To sieve a hard-cooked egg for a garnish or decoration, as strange as it may sound, press the egg through a strainer. This will finely shred the white and yolk. Sprinkle on top of salads or steamed vegetables. Or, gently grate the egg on a fine grater. (Watch your fingers.)*

$\underline{8}$ Steamed Fresh Vegetables

½ pound thin asparagus (if thick, halve lengthwise)

2 medium carrots, peeled, cut into 2- × -¼-inch matchsticks*

2 cups broccoli florets

1 medium yellow squash or zucchini, cut into 2- × -2½-inch chunks

3 tablespoons butter

2 to 3 tablespoons chopped fresh basil, dill, or parsley

2 to 3 tablespoons chopped scallions

Salt and freshly ground black pepper

SERVES 4 AS A SIDE DISH

This recipe includes four vegetables, colorful and complementary in flavor and texture, "steam-cooked" in very little water. If one is not available, double up on another.

1   Trim and discard the woody ends from the asparagus.* Cut into 2-inch lengths.

2   In a deep covered skillet, heat 1 inch of lightly salted water to a boil. Add all the vegetables except the squash. Return to a boil. Cover and steam 1 minute; add the squash. Steam 3 minutes longer, until vegetables are crisp-tender. Drain.

3   Melt the butter in the same skillet. Return the vegetables and toss with the basil, dill, or parsley; the scallions; salt; and freshly ground black pepper to taste. Serve immediately.

Tip   * To cut matchstick pieces of carrot or other vegetables, peel carrot. Cut into 2-inch lengths. Put each piece on end. Carefully slice down, with a chef's knife, into ¼-inch strips. Stack a few strips and cut lengthwise into sticks.

Variation 1 VEGETABLES À LA RUSSE

SERVES 4

These are steamed and tossed with a mayonnaise dressing. Serve as a first course, side dish or salad course.

Make STEAMED FRESH VEGETABLES with the following changes: Rinse the steamed vegetables quickly under cold water to stop cooking; drain well. Omit the butter. Toss with the basil, scallions, and *½ to ⅔ cup Green Herb Dressing*, or sprinkle with *oil, vinegar,* salt, and freshly ground black pepper.

Variation 2 AU GRATIN VEGETABLES

SERVES 4 TO 6 AS A SIDE DISH

Make STEAMED FRESH VEGETABLES with the following changes: Heat the oven to 375°. Make STEAMED FRESH VEGETABLES, omitting the butter, salt, and pepper. Make *1 recipe Cheese Sauce.* Transfer the vegetables to a 12- × -8-inch oval gratin dish or a 1½-quart shallow baking dish. Pour on the sauce. Sprinkle with *2 tablespoons plain bread crumbs.* Bake 25 minutes, until bubbling and golden.

Variation 3 STIR-FRY

4 SERVINGS

Make STEAMED FRESH VEGETABLES with the following changes: Cut raw vegetables for STEAMED FRESH VEGETABLES. Do not cook. Omit the butter and seasonings. Toast *¼ cup sesame seeds* in a nonstick skillet over low heat about 5 minutes, until golden and fragrant. In a small bowl, stir *2 tablespoons soy sauce; 1 tablespoon lemon juice; 2 teaspoons minced fresh ginger; 1 clove garlic, minced; and ¼ teaspoon sugar.* In a 12-inch skillet or wok, heat *2 tablespoons olive oil* over high heat. Add all the vegetables, except the squash. Stir-fry* 1 minute; add the squash. Stir-fry 2 minutes more. Pour in soy mixture. Stir-fry 1 minute, until vegetables are tender. Toss with sesame seeds. Serve as a side dish.

Tips
Asparagus spears have a natural "breaking" point. Hold each uncooked spear with one hand in the middle and the other at the stem end. Snap the spear. It will break at the right point. Discard the woody end.

To stir-fry, hold a wooden spoon or fork, or a Chinese metal spatula in each hand. When oil is hot, add the vegetables. With one hand at "three o'clock" and one at "nine o'clock" bring the utensils to the center, lifting the vegetables. Continue bringing the outside vegetables to the center. There should be constant motion to insure even cooking.

17

9 *Fresh Tomato Sauce*

2 large ripe tomatoes, about 8
ounces each

½ cup tomato or vegetable juice

½ medium red onion, minced

¼ cup slivered fresh basil leaves

2 tablespoons olive oil

1 clove garlic, minced

½ teaspoon salt

Freshly ground black pepper

MAKES ABOUT 3 CUPS

*This recipe provides the perfect solution to the problem of a surplus of
juicy, red, ripe tomatoes. Tossed over hot pasta with slivers of fresh
Parmesan cheese or spooned over chicken cutlets or fish, it is an uncooked, light and refreshing summer sauce with a coarse and chunky
texture.*

1 Core the tomatoes; cut into ½-inch chunks. Transfer to a
   bowl.

2 Toss with the remaining ingredients. Let stand at least 30
   minutes, tossing occasionally to blend flavors.

18

Variation 1   **C**HUNKY TOMATO SALAD

Make FRESH TOMATO SAUCE with the following changes: Omit the ½ cup tomato juice. Let stand 30 minutes. Spoon over shredded iceberg lettuce.

Variation 2   **G**AZPACHO SOUP

Make FRESH TOMATO SAUCE with the following changes: Use *2 cups tomato juice*; substitute *fresh mint* for the basil, or use a combination. Stir in *1 cup diced peeled cucumber; ½ a green bell pepper, diced; and 2 tablespoons red wine vinegar.* In the container of a food processor or blender, puree half the mixture, in batches, if necessary. Stir into the remaining mixture. Refrigerate several hours. Serve.

Variation 3   **S**ALSA

If you don't like the heat, omit the cayenne pepper. Serve with tortilla chips as an hors d' oeuvre; spoon over Chicken Fajitas, Beef Fajitas, or serve with Educated Shrimp Cocktail.

Make FRESH TOMATO SAUCE with the following changes: Substitute *2 tablespoons chopped cilantro* for the basil. Stir in *1 tablespoon fresh lime juice; ½ a green bell pepper, finely chopped; ¼ teaspoon each ground cumin and cayenne pepper.* Let stand at least 30 minutes.

10 White Sauce/Béchamel

A velvety WHITE SAUCE (see Secrets of a Competent Cook, page 68), also called BÉCHAMEL, will drape casually over vegetables, mashed potatoes, or over fish. Whisk it slowly and carefully, as though you had all the time in the world.

3 tablespoons butter
3 tablespoons flour
2 cups milk
½ teaspoon salt
Freshly ground black pepper

MAKES ABOUT 2 CUPS

1 In a heavy saucepan, melt the butter* over low heat, until foamy. With a wooden spoon, stir in the flour until a thin paste forms. This is called a "roux."

2 Whisk in the milk until smooth. Stirring occasionally, cook 10 to 12 minutes, until simmering, thick, and smooth. Simmer 2 minutes to "cook out" the flour taste.

3 Season with the salt and freshly ground black pepper.

Variation **1** $\boldsymbol{C}$**HEESE SAUCE**   MAKES ABOUT 2 CUPS

Serve this over broccoli, cauliflower, or Mashed Potato Croquettes.

Make WHITE SAUCE with the following changes: Stir in about 1 cup (4 ounces) shredded sharp Cheddar cheese, off the heat, until smooth.

Variation **2** $\boldsymbol{H}$**ERB SAUCE**   MAKES ABOUT 2 CUPS

Serve over cooked vegetables, fish, or chicken.

Make WHITE SAUCE with the following changes: Stir in ¼ *cup chopped fresh parsley, dill, chives, scallions, or basil* at the last minute.

Variation **3** $\boldsymbol{C}$**HICKEN GRAVY**   MAKES ABOUT 2 CUPS

Make WHITE SAUCE with the following changes: Substitute *1 cup chicken broth* for 1 cup milk. (If you are roasting a chicken, stir *1 to 2 tablespoons of the pan drippings* into the Chicken Gravy at the last minute.)

Tip   * *If you brown the butter slightly after it has melted (don't burn it!), it will add a nutty flavor to the sauce.*

11 Salad Dressing

1/3 cup olive oil

1/3 cup vegetable oil

3 tablespoons vinegar of your choice

2 tablespoons mayonnaise

1 tablespoon water

2 teaspoons Dijon mustard

1/4 to 1/2 teaspoon salt

1/4 teaspoon sugar

Freshly ground black pepper

Fresh parsley or chives, chopped (optional)

MAKES 1 GENEROUS CUP

Use any combination of vegetable, peanut, olive, or other oils that you prefer; or use only one oil. A mixture of olive and vegetable makes a light-tasting dressing. A fruity dark olive oil will make a stronger-tasting dressing.

1   In a small covered jar, shake all the ingredients, until the mixture is smooth.

2   Let stand at least 30 minutes for the flavors to develop.

Variation 1 *O*RIENTAL SESAME DRESSING

MAKES ABOUT 1½ CUPS

Serve the Oriental Sesame Dressing on a bean sprout salad, over shredded cooked chicken, sliced steak, Thai Beef Salad, or on cold linguini to make cold sesame noodles.

Make SALAD DRESSING with the following changes: Toast *¼ cup sesame seeds* in a nonstick skillet over low heat about 5 minutes, until golden and fragrant. Prepare SALAD DRESSING. Omit the salt. Stir in *1 tablespoon soy sauce*, *¼ cup peanut butter*, and *¼ cup sliced scallions*, until smooth. Stir in the sesame seeds.

Variation 2 *G*REEN HERB DRESSING

MAKES ABOUT 1¼ CUPS

The Green Herb Dressing can be a dip for assorted crudités as well as a dressing for mixed greens or sliced tomatoes. Substitute basil, chives, or tarragon for the dill; or use a mixture of assorted fresh herbs. If you have little pots of kitchen herbs on your windowsill, or an herb garden, snip little ends off the plants, rinse, and toss into the dressing.

Make SALAD DRESSING with the following changes: Substitute *⅔ cup (total) mayonnaise* for the oils, *2 tablespoons lemon juice* for the vinegar. In a food processor or blender, puree the dressing with *1 cup loosely packed watercress leaves, 3 tablespoons sliced scallions, and 1 tablespoon chopped fresh dill.*

Variation 3 *R*OQUEFORT OR GOAT CHEESE DRESSING

MAKES ABOUT 1½ CUPS

Serve the Roquefort or Goat Cheese Dressing on a substantial green—with endive and watercress, or over arugula or chicory.

Make SALAD DRESSING with the following changes: Substitute *⅔ cup sour cream or plain yogurt or a combination* for the oils and *1 tablespoon lemon juice* for the vinegar. Omit the mustard, salt, and sugar. Whisk in *½ cup (2 ounces) crumbled Roquefort or goat cheese*, or puree in a food processor or blender until smooth.

Tip   * *Store salad dressings in a covered jar in the refrigerator. Shake well before using.*

12 Sautéed Chicken Cutlets

1/4 cup flour

1/2 teaspoon salt

Freshly ground black pepper

4 boneless, skinless chicken breast halves, about 1 1/4 pounds

1 tablespoon olive oil

1 tablespoon butter

1 tablespoon chopped fresh parsley

Thin slices of lemon

SERVES 4

These cutlets are very simple and very quick to prepare.

1 Combine the flour, salt, and pepper.

2 Dredge the chicken on all sides in the seasoned flour. Shake off any excess.

3 In a large skillet, heat the oil and butter over medium heat.

4 Saute the chicken 8 to 10 minutes, turning* 2 or 3 times, until golden, lightly crusted, and cooked through.

5 Sprinkle with chopped parsley and garnish with sliced lemon.

Variation **1** ***C*HICKEN FLORENTINE** SERVES 4

The hot gravy coats the chicken and wilts the spinach.

Make SAUTÉED CHICKEN CUTLETS with the following changes: Wash *8 cups loosely packed fresh spinach leaves* with stems removed. Dry well. Stack and cut the spinach in very fine strips. Arrange on each of 4 plates. Make *1 recipe Chicken Gravy;* keep warm. Cook the chicken as above. Place 1 cutlet on the spinach on each plate. Spoon the gravy over the chicken and spinach. Sprinkle with parsley and garnish with lemon, if desired.

Variation **2** ***C*HICKEN FAJITAS** SERVES 4

These cutlets are marinated first. Serve with Mexican Salsa and Cold Rice Salad.

Make SAUTÉED CHICKEN CUTLETS with the following changes: In a small bowl, stir *the juice of 1 lime, ½ teaspoon chili powder, ½ teaspoon ground cumin, ¼ teaspoon garlic powder, ¼ teaspoon salt, and freshly ground black pepper.* Rub this mixture on the chicken; marinate 1 hour. Flour and sauté the cutlets as above. Slice each cutlet diagonally in 4 or 6 pieces. Omit the parsley and lemon.

Variation **3** ***L*EMON PEPPER CHICKEN** SERVES 4

Make SAUTÉED CHICKEN CUTLETS with the following changes: In a bowl, sprinkle the chicken with *2 teaspoons cracked black pepper, grated rind of 1 lemon, and ¼ teaspoon salt.* Let stand 30 minutes. Flour and sauté the cutlets as above. Remove the chicken and pour off the fat in the skillet. Add the *juice of 1 lemon* to the pan, shaking and scraping up any bits that cling to the bottom. Slice each cutlet diagonally in 4 or 6 pieces. Arrange on a platter. Pour on the pan juices. Sprinkle with parsley and garnish with lemon. Serve immediately or at room temperature.

Tip   ** Use wooden or metal kitchen tongs for turning chicken cutlets. Do not pierce them with a fork; you will release the juices.*

25

13 Broiled Flank Steak

Flank steak is a versatile cut of beef. On some parts of the planet it is known as London Broil. Quickly broiled, thinly sliced across the grain and on an angle, it is a tender and tasty steak.

1 flank steak, about 1¼ pounds

1 tablespoon olive oil

Salt and freshly ground black pepper

SERVES 4

1   Brush the steak with oil.

2   Heat a broiler pan 5 minutes under the broiler.

3   Place the steak on the pan and broil about 4 minutes per side for medium rare.

4   Transfer to a cutting board. Let stand about 5 minutes. Cut very thin slices against the grain and on an angle. Sprinkle with salt and pepper.

Variation **1** **B**EEF FAJITAS   SERVES 4

Serve with warm flour tortillas and Mexican Salsa.

Make BROILED FLANK STEAK with the following changes: In a shallow bowl, stir the oil; *2 tablespoons fresh squeezed lime juice; 2 tablespoons minced onion; 2 cloves garlic, minced; ½ teaspoon ground cumin; salt, and freshly ground black pepper*. Coat the steak with this mixture. Let stand 1 hour. Cook and slice.

Variation **2** **T**HAI BEEF SALAD   SERVES 4 TO 6

Make BROILED FLANK STEAK with the following changes: Rub the flank steak with a small amount of *soy sauce and oil*. Broil and slice as above. Omit the salt and pepper. In a large bowl, toss *½ pound blanched green beans*; ¼ medium red cabbage, coarsely shredded; ½ medium cucumber, cut into long thin strips; ½ medium red onion, cut into thin strips; 1 recipe Oriental Sesame Dressing*; and the sliced steak.

Variation **3** **R**OLLED FLANK STEAK   SERVES 4

This steak is rolled up and tied before baking. To serve, arrange overlapping slices on a platter. Serve warm, at room temperature, or cold with SALAD DRESSING.

Make BROILED FLANK STEAK with the following changes: Heat oven to 350°. With a thin, sharp knife, score one side of steak in a crisscross pattern, cutting ¼ to ½ inch deep (see illustration).
Do not cut through to other side. Rub *1 tablespoon tomato paste* into scored meat. In a small bowl, toss *¼ cup grated Parmesan cheese; ¼ cup slivered fresh basil leaves; 3 tablespoons plain bread crumbs; 1 clove garlic, minced;* salt, and pepper. Sprinkle mixture over and into scored surface of meat. Starting with a long side, roll up meat. With a 48-inch string, tie a loop around one end. Coil the remaining string around the roll to opposite end. Tie to secure. Rub meat with *1 teaspoon olive oil*. Put in a small baking pan. Bake 30 minutes for medium rare. Let stand 15 minutes. Remove string. Cut into ½-inch slices.

Tip   ** To blanch green beans, cook the beans, covered, in a small amount of boiling salted water about 4 to 5 minutes, until crisp but tender. Plunge the beans into a bowl of cold water to stop the cooking. Drain well.*

27

14 Meat Loaf

4 slices raw bacon, cut into
1/2-inch pieces

1 1/4 pounds ground beef
or turkey, or a mixture

1/2 cup canned or homemade
tomato or marinara sauce

1/2 cup plain bread crumbs

1/2 cup chopped onion

1/4 cup finely chopped celery

1 clove garlic, minced

1/2 teaspoon dried oregano leaves

1/4 teaspoon salt

Freshly ground black pepper

SERVES 4 TO 6

1 Heat the oven to 325°.

2 In a skillet, fry the bacon over medium heat 5 to 7 minutes, until crisp. Pour off all but 1 tablespoon fat.

3 In a 1 1/2- or 2-quart casserole, using your hands, mix all the ingredients with the bacon and reserved tablespoon of fat, until well blended. Do not overmix. It will toughen the meat loaf.

4 Shape into an 8-inch loaf in the casserole.

5 Bake 1 hour. Let stand 5 minutes. Pour off the fat. Slice and serve.

Variation **1** P̂ÂTÉ

MAKES ABOUT 16 ½-INCH SLICES

Pâté is essentially a meat loaf, but all gussied up. Serve as an hors d'oeuvre with mustard, chutney, or gherkins.

Make MEAT LOAF with the following changes: Heat oven to 325°. Omit bread crumbs. Substitute *½ cup heavy cream* for tomato sauce and *½ teaspoon dried thyme leaves, crumbled* for oregano. Increase the salt to ½ teaspoon. Stir in *one 10-ounce package frozen chopped spinach, thawed and squeezed dry* and *¼ teaspoon ground allspice.* Shape and bake as above. Cool. Pour off fat. Wrap and refrigerate several hours or preferably overnight. Slice and serve.

Variation **2** OUR '21' BURGER

SERVES 4

When I called the '21' Club and asked about the recipe for their special burger, Executive Chef Michael Lomonaco invited me to tour his kitchens. My recipe is based on a burger once served at this famous restaurant.

Make MEAT LOAF with the following changes: Heat the oven to 375°. Fry the bacon 5 minutes. Add the onion, celery, and garlic to the skillet. Cook 5 minutes. Pour off all but 1 tablespoon fat. Cool the mixture slightly. In a bowl, mix the ground beef, *¼ cup plain bread crumbs,* salt, and freshly ground black pepper. Omit the herb and tomato sauce. Blend in the bacon mixture. Do not overmix. Shape into four 3½-inch patties. In a heavy ovenproof skillet, heat *1 tablespoon olive oil* over high heat until very hot. Brown the burgers 2 minutes per side, sprinkling each with *a few drops of Worcestershire sauce.* Transfer the skillet to the oven. Cook about 6 to 8 minutes for medium rare. Let stand 2 minutes. Serve on poppy-seed rolls.

Variation **3** CHILI

SERVES 4 TO 6

Serve with sour cream and chopped onion.

Make MEAT LOAF with the following changes: In a 5-quart pot, fry the bacon as above. Pour off all but *2 tablespoons fat.* Stir in the onion, celery, and garlic. Omit the bread crumbs. Cook 5 minutes. Crumble in the ground beef. Cook 5 minutes, stirring, until browned. Stir in *2 teaspoons chili powder, 1 teaspoon ground cumin,* the oregano, *¼ teaspoon cayenne pepper,* the salt, and freshly ground black pepper. Cook 5 minutes. Stir in *2½ cups (total) tomato sauce and one 16-ounce can kidney beans, drained (about 2 cups).* Cover and cook 20 minutes, stirring occasionally. Let stand 5 minutes. Season with salt and pepper.

15 Omelet

An omelet should be light in color and texture, fluffy, airy, and a little moist on the inside. It should have height when served, even if there is no filling. Making an omelet is not difficult, but it does take a little practice.

TO MAKE A PROPER OMELET: If you hold this book in one hand and try to make an omelet with two other hands, you are in trouble. If you set the book down and read while you are making the omelet, the eggs will cook faster than you could ever read. Alas, the answer is practice and a bit of coordination. Keep the eggs moving. Remember, you may lose an omelet or two before your first triumph.

Some cooks have set aside a particular pan for omelets only. ("Don't you dare cook a hamburger in my omelet pan!") They take great care in wiping it out and oiling it lightly after each use, to "season" the surface and keep it smooth. An omelet pan is a kitchen treasure; however, any 8-inch nonstick skillet is a great substitute and requires less care.

2 eggs
⅛ teaspoon salt
Freshly ground black pepper
1 tablespoon olive oil

SERVES 1

1   Heat the broiler. In a small bowl, using a fork, lightly beat the eggs, salt, and pepper.

2   In an 8-inch nonstick oven-proof skillet, heat the oil over a medium-high flame until hot (a drop of water will sizzle). Swirl the pan to coat the bottom and sides in hot oil.

3   Pour in the egg mixture. Let it cook about 30 seconds; the edges will puff and bubble slightly and just begin to set. Hold the skillet handle with one hand, a wooden spoon with the other. Make "figure eights" with the spoon, starting at twelve o'clock, then three o'clock, etc., pushing the cooked edges toward the center and letting the uncooked egg run to the sides. Keep the eggs moving until the bottom is set and the top is slightly moist.

4   Place the skillet under the broiler 30 seconds to 1 minute, until the eggs are puffed and cooked to your liking. Slide half the omelet onto a plate and invert the pan to fold over the remaining half.

Variation 1   **O**MELET FINES HERBES

SERVES 1

This classic French omelet adds minced fresh herbs to the beaten eggs.

Make the OMELET with the following changes: Using a fork, beat *1 tablespoon minced fresh herbs* (any combination of dill, basil, parsley, chives, or tarragon) into the egg mixture. Prepare as above.

Variation 2   **C**HEDDAR-TOMATO OMELET

SERVES 1

Make the OMELET with the following changes: In a small bowl, toss *½ ripe plum tomato, diced,* and *¼ cup shredded sharp Cheddar cheese.* * Sprinkle the filling over half the omelet before broiling. Fold and serve.

Variation 3   **D**ELI AND EGGS

SERVES 1

Use any deli meat—corned beef, pastrami, ham, roast beef, salami or bologna—for this egg pancake. Serve with rye toast and a half-sour pickle.

Make the OMELET with the following changes: Heat the oil in the skillet. Sauté *1 ounce deli meat, slivered (about ¼ cup)* and *2 tablespoons sliced scallions* 2 minutes. Pour on the eggs and cook as above. Slide onto a plate. Do not fold.

Tips   ** For the Cheddar, substitute any melting cheese, such as mozzarella, Jarlsberg, Monterey Jack, Fontina, Brie (skin removed), Swiss, or Gruyère.*

* Double any OMELET recipe and cook in a 10-inch skillet to serve 2 or 3.

Pasta Primavera

8 ounces large bow ties or other pasta of your choice

1 recipe STEAMED FRESH VEGETABLES

½ cup heavy cream

½ cup chicken broth

¼ cup grated Parmesan cheese, plus additional at table

Salt and freshly ground black pepper

SERVES 4

Whether it is an American invention or an Italian classic is not really the point. This dish is simple, light, and delicious.

1   Cook the pasta according to the package directions. Drain. Return to the pot.

2   While the pasta is cooking, prepare the STEAMED FRESH VEGETABLES. Add to the pasta.

3   In a deep skillet, simmer the cream, broth, and cheese until slightly thickened. Pour over the pasta and vegetables. Season with salt and freshly ground black pepper.

4   Toss over low heat until the pasta is heated through and coated in sauce. Serve with additional cheese.

Variation 1 *P*ASTA PRIMAVERA SALAD

SERVES 2

Serve this salad at room temperature or refrigerate and serve cold.

Make PASTA PRIMAVERA with the following changes: Omit the cream and broth. Cook *4 ounces pasta*. Rinse and drain. Cook half the recipe for STEAMED FRESH VEGETABLES, omitting the butter. In a large bowl, toss the pasta, vegetables, *1 ripe medium tomato, cut into chunks; ¼ cup shaved Parmesan cheese; 2 tablespoons olive oil; 1 tablespoon lemon juice; ¼ teaspoon salt; and freshly ground black pepper.*

Variation 2 *M*ACARONI AND CHEESE

SERVES 6

This old-fashioned favorite appears in a new outfit, full of spring green (and yellow and orange).

Make PASTA PRIMAVERA with the following changes: Omit the cream and broth. Heat the oven to 375°. Cook the pasta; make half the recipe for STEAMED FRESH VEGETABLES. Make *1½ recipes (about 3 cups) Cheese Sauce*. In a *buttered* 2½-quart casserole, stir the pasta, vegetables, and sauce. Sprinkle the top with *2 tablespoons grated Parmesan cheese and 2 tablespoons plain bread crumbs.* Bake 30 minutes, until golden and bubbling.

Variation 3 *C*HUNKY MINESTRONE SOUP

MAKES 7 CUPS

Make PASTA PRIMAVERA with the following changes: Omit the heavy cream. In a soup pot, heat *5 cups (total) chicken broth; 1 tablespoon tomato paste; 1 clove garlic, minced; and 1 teaspoon olive oil* to a boil. Cook *2 ounces pasta of your choice* in the broth, partially covered, until al dente (firm). Prepare half the recipe for STEAMED FRESH VEGETABLES, omitting the butter. Cook the vegetables in the broth with *1 cup canned drained chick-peas*. Heat to a simmer. Cover and cook 5 minutes, until the vegetables are tender. Season with salt and freshly gound black pepper. Sprinkle *1 tablespoon grated Parmesan cheese* over each serving.

17 **R**oast Chicken

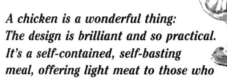

A chicken is a wonderful thing:
The design is brilliant and so practical.
It's a self-contained, self-basting
meal, offering light meat to those who
prefer, dark to others, and a delight to those who eat everything. Toss it
casually into the oven. Out will emerge a golden, succulent, and aromatic
bird. Everyone will know somethng wonderful is coming to the table.

1   Heat the oven to 375°.

2   Place the chicken, breast side up, in a small roasting pan or shallow casserole*. Sprinkle with salt and pepper, if desired.

3   Roast 30 minutes. Lower heat to 350°. Roast 30 to 35 minutes more, until golden and juices run clear when thickest part of thigh is pierced.

4   Remove from the oven. Let stand 10 to 15 minutes. Carve (see How To Cut Up a Whole Roast Chicken, page 69) and serve. Spoon any pan juices over the carved meat.

1 whole roasting chicken,
about 3 pounds
Salt and freshly ground black
pepper (optional)

SERVES 2 TO 4

Variation **1** **O**RIENTAL CHICKEN

SERVES 2 TO 4

Though this calls for ½ teaspoon cayenne pepper, the chicken meat is pleasantly spiced, the skin is hotter.

Make ROAST CHICKEN with the following changes: In a small bowl, stir _2 tablespoons soy sauce; 2 teaspoons lemon juice; 2 or 3 cloves garlic, minced; 2 to 3 teaspoons minced or grated fresh ginger; ½ teaspoon cayenne pepper; and ½ teaspoon sugar._ Pour this mixture over the uncooked chicken. Rub it thoroughly over the chicken and under the breast skin*. Place in a large bowl and let stand, loosely covered, about 1½ hours, turning over 3 or 4 times. (If your kitchen is warm, marinate in the refrigerator.) Roast as above.

Variation **2** **D**IJON CHICKEN TARRAGON

SERVES 2 TO 4

Make ROAST CHICKEN with the following changes: In a small bowl, stir _2 tablespoons Dijon mustard, 2 tablespoons minced shallots, 1 teaspoon dried tarragon, and freshly ground black pepper._ Rub this mixture thoroughly over the uncooked chicken and under the breast skin*. Place in a large bowl and let stand, loosely covered, about 1 hour. Roast as above.

Variation **3** **O**UR CHICKEN KIEV

SERVES 2 TO 4

Make ROAST CHICKEN with the following changes: In a small bowl, stir _4 tablespoons softened butter; 3 tablespoons chopped chives (or scallions); 3 tablespoons chopped fresh dill; 2 cloves garlic, minced; ¾ teaspoon paprika; ¼ teaspoon salt; and freshly ground black pepper._ Rub this mixture thoroughly over the uncooked chicken and under the breast skin*. Place in a large bowl and refrigerate, covered, about 1 hour. Bake as above.

Tips * _Half a lemon or onion, a stalk of celery, whole cloves of garlic, or fresh herb sprigs can be placed in the cavity before baking to add flavor. Discard before serving._

* _To spread an herb or spice mixture under the breast skin of a whole chicken, gently separate the skin from the flesh with your fingers. Start from the cavity end. Run your fingers gently under the skin to separate._

* _Try serving ROAST CHICKEN with Chicken Gravy._

18 Roast Loin of Pork

Have the butcher bone out a 3½-pound pork loin, trimming, cracking, and saving the bones, to yield a 2-pound boneless roast, tied. Place the bones in a shallow casserole to act as a "cradle" for the loin as it roasts. Otherwise, make a "bed" of celery tops and sliced carrots.

4 teaspoons soy sauce

1 teaspoon sugar

1 teaspoon cracked black pepper

½ teaspoon salt

1 boneless loin of pork, tied, about 2 pounds (see above)

SERVES 4 TO 5

1 Heat oven to 325°.

2 In a small bowl, stir the soy sauce, sugar, pepper, and salt. Pour this mixture over the loin and rub it in.

3 Place the loin, fat side up, on the bones, vegetables (see above), or on a small rack in a baking dish. Roast, uncovered, 1 hour and 45 minutes. Add a few tablespoons water if the bottom of the pan is dry. The pork should be cooked to an internal temperature of 155°. It will continue cooking after it is removed from the oven. Remove from the oven when it reaches just under 155°.*

4 Cover and let stand 5 minutes.

5 Slice the loin and serve (with the bones if you have them).

Variation 1 **G**ARLIC ROAST PORK

Make ROAST LOIN OF PORK with the following changes: Finely chop *10 to 12 cloves of garlic.* Stir into the soy mixture. Pour the mixture over the loin and rub it in, leaving most of the garlic on top. Roast as above.

Variation 2 **N**ORMANDY ROAST PORK WITH GINGER

Make ROAST LOIN OF PORK with the following changes: Place the soy-seasoned loin in a baking dish, as above. Peel and core *3 tart baking apples.* Cut each one in 8 wedges and crosswise in quarters. Toss in a bowl with *1 small onion, coarsely chopped, and 1 tablespoon minced fresh ginger.* Spoon the apple mixture around the roast. Roast as above, stirring the apples occasionally; add *¼ cup apple juice, cider, or water,* if the mixture looks dry. Slice the pork and serve the apples on the side.

Variation **3** ***C*URRIED PORK STEW**

A boneless loin of pork is not the most practical cut for stew. It tends to dry out. Instead, buy a 2-pound boneless shoulder roast and cut it in 1½-inch cubes. You may substitute shoulder of veal or veal stew meat.

Make ROAST LOIN OF PORK with the following changes: Omit the soy, sugar, and cracked pepper. In a large, heavy soup pot, brown* the *cubed pork* in *1 to 2 tablespoons olive oil,* in batches, if necessary. Set aside. Add *another tablespoon of oil* to the pan. Stir in ½ *cup chopped onion;* ½ *cup chopped celery; 1 clove garlic, minced; 2 teaspoons curry powder;* ½ *teaspoon ground cumin;* and ¼ *teaspoon cayenne pepper.* Cook 5 minutes. Stir in the pork, 2½ *cups chicken broth,* ½ *cup tomato sauce,* ½ *cup raisins, 1 2 × ½ inch strip of lemon rind, and a pinch of salt.* Heat to a boil. Lower the heat, cover, and simmer 1¼ to 1½ hours, until tender. Partially uncover after 1 hour. Serve with Middle Eastern Pilau.

Tips   * *Buy an "instant-read" meat thermometer. Ten minutes before the recommended cooking time has elapsed, insert the thermometer through the top of the roast into the center. The dial will stop at the internal temperature.*

* *To brown meat for a stew, heat the oil until hot. Add the cubed meat in batches. Don't crowd the meat or it will "steam," give off its juices, and dry out. Sear the cubes, turning them until golden on all sides, to retain the natural juices.*

19 Shrimp Scampi

1¼ pounds raw medium
shrimp, peeled and deveined*

2 tablespoons olive oil

2 cloves garlic, minced

1 teaspoon freshly grated
lemon rind

½ teaspoon salt

Freshly ground black pepper

Pinch of cayenne pepper
(optional)

SERVES 4

I'm not sure why, but nearly everyone (except my brother) loves shrimp.

1   In a large bowl, toss the shrimp with the remaining ingredients. Marinate, loosely covered, 1 hour.

2   Heat a large cast-iron skillet or wok over high heat, until very hot.

3   Add the shrimp all at once and stir-fry* 2 minutes, until the shrimp curl and are cooked through. Serve immediately.

Variation 1   *E*DUCATED SHRIMP COCKTAIL

Make SHRIMP SCAMPI with the following changes: When peeling the shrimp, leave the shell on the tail portions for easy serving. Marinate and cook as above. Cool slightly and refrigerate until cold. Arrange decoratively on a platter. Serve with Mexican Salsa or Green Herb Dressing.

Variation 2   *L*IGHT SHRIMP SALAD

SERVES 4

Make SHRIMP SCAMPI with the following changes: While shrimp marinates, in a large bowl, toss *½ cup cooked green peas; ½ small red onion, cut into strips; 2 plum tomatoes, cut into 8 wedges; 2 tablespoons olive oil; 1 tablespoon fresh lime juice; 1 tablespoon chopped cilantro or parsley; ¼ teaspoon salt; and freshly ground black pepper.* Cook the SHRIMP SCAMPI then add the hot shrimp to the salad. Toss until well blended. Cool to room temperature. Just before serving, toss in *½ medium-size ripe avocado, cut into chunks.*

Variation 3   *S*HRIMP PAELLA

SERVES 4

Make SHRIMP SCAMPI with the following changes: Marinate the shrimp for 1 hour. Make *1 recipe Spanish Rice.* Transfer the rice to a large baking dish and keep warm in a low (300°) oven. Cook SHRIMP SCAMPI. Arrange the shrimp over the rice. Serve immediately, sprinkled with *chopped parsley.*

Tips   * *To devein the shrimp, peel off and discard the shells. With a paring knife, cut a shallow slit the full length of the back of the shrimp. Scrape or pull out the dark vein and discard.*

     * *To stir-fry, see STEAMED FRESH VEGETABLES, Tips (page 17).*

20 Simple Sole

These recipes are quick and easy and the perfect choice for a last-minute dinner for two, providing you have the fish. They are ideally suited to microwave cooking but work equally well in a conventional oven (see Tips).

Use any firm-fleshed white fillet, such as sole, flounder, catfish, haddock, or snapper. These recipes call for very thin and flat fillets that can be folded.

2 tablespoons plain bread crumbs

1 tablespoon melted butter

¼ teaspoon paprika

2 small sole fillets, about 5 ounces each

Salt and freshly ground black pepper

½ lemon

SERVES 2

1   In a small bowl, stir the bread crumbs, butter, and paprika.

2   Lightly season the fish with salt and pepper.

3   Fold each fillet in half crosswise. Pat half the crumb mixture on top of each fillet. Arrange the 2 fillets on a microwave-safe plate, the thicker portions toward the edge of the plate. Cover loosely with plastic wrap.

4   Microwave on HIGH 3 minutes. Let stand 30 seconds. Gently lift the plastic. Squeeze on the lemon and serve.

Variation 1 STUFFED SOLE

SERVES 2

Make SIMPLE SOLE with the following changes: In a small skillet, sauté *¼ cup each minced onion, carrot, and mushrooms* in *1 tablespoon butter* over low heat about 5 minutes. Season the vegetables lightly with *salt and pepper*. Cool slightly. Spoon the vegetables over half of each seasoned fillet before folding. Top the fish with the crumb mixture and microwave *3½* minutes, as above.* Squeeze the lemon over the fish and serve.

Variation 2 STUFFED SOLE PROVENÇALE

SERVES 2

Make SIMPLE SOLE with the following changes: Rub both sides of *a slice of white or wheat toast* with *1 whole clove garlic, peeled*. Cut the bread into ½-inch cubes. In a bowl, toss the bread with *½ cup diced tomato (fresh or canned); 4 imported black olives, pitted and slivered; 1 tablespoon each chopped fresh basil and scallion*. Spoon the stuffing over half of each seasoned fillet before folding. Top the fish with the crumb mixture and microwave *3½* minutes, as above.* Squeeze the lemon over the fish and serve.

Variation 3 STUFFED CAJUN SOLE

SERVES 2

Make SIMPLE SOLE with the following changes: In a small skillet, sauté in *1 tablespoon olive oil ½ cup diced zucchini; 1 tablespoon chopped shallot or onion; ¼ teaspoon dried thyme leaves; a pinch each of salt, freshly ground black pepper, and cayenne pepper* for 2 to 3 minutes. Rub both sides of a *slice of white or wheat toast* with *1 whole clove garlic, peeled*. Cut the bread into ½-inch cubes. In a bowl, toss the bread with the vegetables. Spoon the stuffing over half of each seasoned fillet before folding. Stir *¼ teaspoon dried oregano leaves and ⅛ teaspoon cayenne pepper* into the crumb mixture. Top the fish with the crumbs and microwave *3½ minutes*, as above.* Squeeze the lemon over the fish and serve.

Tip * *To cook any of these recipes in a conventional oven, heat the oven to 450°. Arrange each prepared fillet on half of a 12-inch square of foil (one square for each fillet). Fold over the remaining half and crimp the edges to seal. Place the 2 packets on a baking sheet. Bake 15 minutes. The sealed packets allow the fish to steam in its natural juices.*

45

Apple Pie

Crust

2½ cups flour

1 tablespoon sugar

Pinch of salt

10 tablespoons butter

3 to 4 tablespoons ice water

Filling

4 medium-size tart apples,
such as Granny Smith

½ cup golden raisins

⅓ cup sugar

½ teaspoon ground cinnamon

½ teaspoon vanilla extract

Additional flour for rolling

Sugar for sprinkling

SERVES 8

No one will fall off a dining-room chair when the pie is brought to the table, but there will be low hums and faint nods of approval. And the home in which an apple pie has just been baked is full of the sweet smells of apples and sugar and cinnamon.

1 To make the crust, in a bowl toss the flour, sugar and salt. Using a pastry blender (see How to Stock a Kitchen, page 70), 2 knives, or your fingertips, quickly cut in the butter,* until the mixture resembles coarse crumbs. Sprinkle on the ice water 1 tablespoon at a time while stirring the mixture just until it can be gathered into a ball. Knead once or twice in the bowl. Divide in half. Wrap each half in plastic or foil and chill 30 minutes.

2 Peel and core the apples*. Cut each apple into 8 wedges. Cut each wedge crosswise into quarters. In a bowl, toss the apples, raisins, sugar, cinnamon, and vanilla.

3 Heat the oven to 350°.

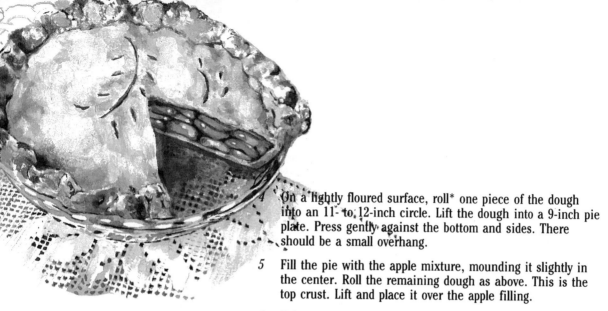

4   On a lightly floured surface, roll* one piece of the dough into an 11- to 12-inch circle. Lift the dough into a 9-inch pie plate. Press gently against the bottom and sides. There should be a small overhang.

5   Fill the pie with the apple mixture, mounding it slightly in the center. Roll the remaining dough as above. This is the top crust. Lift and place it over the apple filling.

6   Crimp or pinch the edges of the top and bottom crusts together around the rim of the pie plate.

7   Brush the top lightly with water. Sprinkle with about 1 teaspoon of sugar. Cut 6 or 8 small slits through the top crust with the tip of a paring knife to allow for the release of steam as the pie bakes.

8   Bake about 1¼ hours, until light golden. Cool slightly before serving.

Variation 1 *A*PPLE STRUDEL

SERVES 8

This is a country-style strudel rolled in a piecrust dough instead of in strudel or filo dough.

Make APPLE PIE with the following changes: Roll all of the dough into a 12- × -10-inch rectangle on a pastry cloth* or a large sheet of plastic wrap. Make half the apple filling. Spoon the filling lengthwise down the center of the dough. Using the cloth or plastic wrap, lift each long edge of dough and fold it over the filling so the 2 edges meet on top. Pinch the edges together. Brush the top lightly with water and sprinkle with *1 teaspoon sugar.* Heat the oven to 350°. Meanwhile, chill the strudel 30 minutes, or until firm to the touch. Using 2 spatulas, lift it off the cloth and onto a *buttered* baking sheet, seam side up. Bake 1 hour, until golden. (The strudel will bake faster on a dark baking sheet.) The filling may leak a bit while baking. Lift the strudel onto a cooling rack. Cool, cut into 8 slices, and serve.

Variation 2 *A*PPLE DUMPLINGS

SERVES 4

Each dumpling is half an apple wrapped and baked in a crust.

Make APPLE PIE with the following changes: Make half the APPLE PIE crust recipe. Chill 30 minutes. Heat the oven to 375°. Halve *2 baking apples* through the stem. Peel and core*. In a small bowl, stir *2 tablespoons golden raisins, 1 tablespoon melted butter, 1 tablespoon sugar, 1/8 teaspoon vanilla extract, and a pinch of ground cinnamon.* Divide the chilled dough into quarters. Roll each piece into a 6-inch square. Place each apple half, cored side up, on a square of dough. Fill or top each with a quarter of the raisin mixture. Bring the corners of the dough up over the tops of the apples so that each is wrapped neatly in the dough. Lightly *butter* a 9-inch pie plate. Arrange the dumplings, seam side up, on the plate. Brush the tops lightly with water and sprinkle with *1 teaspoon sugar.* Bake 30 to 35 minutes, until the dough is golden and the apples are tender when pierced with a knife. Serve warm with *sweetened sour cream or whipped cream.*

48

Variation **3 $\mathcal{A}$PPLE CRUMBLE**

Make APPLE PIE with the following changes: Heat the oven to 350°. Start making the crust, using *1¼ cups flour, 5 tablespoons sugar,* and *¼ teaspoon ground cinnamon.* Cut in *5 tablespoons butter.* Do not add water. The mixture will be crumbly. Make half the apple filling. Spoon the filling into an 8-inch round cake pan. Dot with *2 tablespoons butter.* Pour on *2 tablespoons apple juice or cider.* Sprinkle the flour mixture on top. Bake 45 minutes, until golden and bubbling.

Tips   * *When you "cut in" butter, you are breaking up the pieces of butter while rubbing them into the dry ingredients. The end product is a mass of tiny, buttery, floury nodules. (See also Secrets of a Competent Cook, Pastry, page 68.)*

* *For instructions on how to core the apples, see Secrets of a Competent Cook, page 66.*

* *When rolling out a piecrust dough, you may find it helpful to flatten the dough into a circle and place it between 2 sheets of plastic wrap so it will be easier to lift. When rolling out the dough, roll from the center of the circle out toward the edge, rotating the circle. (Don't roll from the edge toward the center.)*

* *A pastry cloth is a thick cotton square (available in kitchenware stores) designed to make rollling dough easier. Place the cloth on a work surface and flour the cloth lightly. Roll the dough directly on the cloth.*

22 Biscuits

I know biscuits are supposed to be round. Well these aren't. They're square because it's easier. If you've never made biscuits—which are easy to make from scratch—and you find yourself looking at the batter and asking "What is this sticky mess?", you'll know you're on the right track.

1¾ cups flour

1 tablespoon baking powder

1 teaspoon sugar

½ teaspoon salt

8 tablespoons (1 stick) cold butter, cut into 8 or 10 pieces

A scant (slightly less than) ½ cup milk

Additional flour for shaping

MAKES 9 BISCUITS

1   Heat the oven to 450°

2   In a large bowl, toss the flour, baking powder, sugar, and salt.

3   Using a pastry blender (see How to Stock a Kitchen, page 70), 2 knives, or your fingertips, quickly cut in the butter,* until the mixture resembles coarse crumbs.

4   Pour on just enough milk, stirring, for the mixture to form a mass. It may be sticky. Flour your hands and gather into a ball.

5   On a lightly floured surface, with floured fingers, pat the dough into a 6-inch square. Cut into 9 squares. Arrange them 2 to 3 inches apart on a baking sheet.

6   Bake about 14 minutes, until puffed and golden. Serve warm.

51

Variation 1 PEACH AND BERRY SHORTCAKE
MAKES 9

Make BISCUITS with the following additions: In a large bowl, toss *3 ripe medium peaches, peeled,* cut into 8 to 10 wedges, and 2 cups fresh blueberries or raspberries.* (Lightly mash 1 cup.) Add *¼ cup sugar, ¼ teaspoon vanilla extract, and a pinch of ground cinnamon (optional).* Let stand 2 hours, stirring occasionally, until a syrup is formed. Bake BISCUITS, as above. In a separate bowl, stir *2 cups sour cream,* 3 tablespoons sugar, and ½ teaspoon vanilla extract.* Halve the biscuits. Spoon some of the fruit and syrup and a large dollop of cream over the bottom halves. Top with the remaining halves. Spoon on the remaining fruit and cream.

Variation 2 BREAKFAST SCONES
MAKES 9

A tasty snack all day long, these are crisp outside, tender inside.

Make BISCUITS with the following changes: Heat the oven to 425°. Make BISCUITS using *2 tablespoons sugar, only a pinch of salt, and ¼ teaspoon ground cinnamon* in the flour mixture. After the butter is cut in, stir in *½ cup golden raisins* before adding the milk. Shape and cut as above; brush the tops with *1 tablespoon melted butter.* Sprinkle with *1 teaspoon sugar tossed with a pinch of ground cinnamon.* Bake 18 to 20 minutes, until the tops are deep golden and the bottoms lightly browned. Serve warm or at room temperature.

Variation **3** ***P***EACH AND BERRY COBBLER

These individual fruit desserts are delicious served warm or at room temperature. Top each with a small amount of whipped cream.

Make BISCUITS with the following changes: Heat the oven to 400°. Make Peach and Berry Shortcake (see Variation 1, above) *fruit mixture.* Do not let the fruit stand 2 hours; use at once. Divide the fruit among six 10-ounce oven-proof custard cups. Arrange on a baking sheet. Make biscuit dough using *1 cup flour, 1 tablespoon sugar, 1¼ teaspoons baking powder, a pinch of salt, 4 tablespoons butter, and a scant ¼ cup milk.* Drop large spoonfuls of dough over the fruit. Spread with the back of a wet spoon or with wet fingertips to cover the fruit. Brush the tops with *1½ teaspoons melted butter.* Sprinkle with *1 teaspoon sugar tossed with a pinch of ground cinnamon.* Bake 30 minutes, until the tops are golden and the fruit is bubbling. Cool slightly.

Tips   * *To explain the process of cutting in butter, see Secrets of a Competent Cook, Pastry, page 68.*

* *To peel fresh peaches, drop them in boiling water for 1 minute. Plunge them into a bowl of cold water. This will loosen the skin so that you can remove it easily with a paring knife.*

* *Sweetened sour cream is a fine substitute for whipped cream in a shortcake, though certain purists will disagree. It does, however, add a pleasant tang to the dessert and saves you the trouble of whipping cream. Suit yourself. Should you opt for the whipped cream, whip* 1 cup heavy whipping cream with 1 or 2 teaspoons sugar and a drop of vanilla. *(See Secrets of a Competent Cook, page 66.)*

23 Brownies

The once (still?) popular notion
that you can't be too rich or too thin does not apply to
these brownies. Too rich and too thin, they are delicious.

Butter and flour for pan

10 tablespoons butter

8 ounces semisweet chocolate*

¼ cup sour cream

2 teaspoons instant espresso
or coffee powder or granules

1 teaspoon vanilla extract

3 eggs

1 cup sugar

¾ cup flour

MAKES 24 BROWNIES

1 Heat the oven to 350°. Butter and flour a 13-×-9-inch baking pan.* Set aside.

2 Melt the butter and chocolate.* Stir in the sour cream, espresso, and vanilla. Cool to room temperature.

3 With an electric mixer, beat the eggs and sugar, until thick and light.

4 Fold in the cooled chocolate mixture. Fold in the flour in 3 batches, just until the batter is smooth.

5 Spread the mixture into the prepared pan. Bake 18 to 22 minutes, or until a toothpick inserted in the center comes out clean.*

6 Cool in the pan on a rack. Cut into quarters; cut each quarter into 6 brownies.

Tip *Any semisweet or bittersweet chocolate can be used. Semisweet morsels come in 6- and 12-ounce packages. One cup of morsels is equal to 6 ounces. Break up bar chocolate, squares or blocks before melting.*

Variation 1 Peanut Butter Brownies

Make BROWNIES with the following changes: Melt *8 tablespoons (1 stick) butter with 6 ounces chocolate** and *½ cup peanut butter.* Omit the sour cream and instant espresso. Fold in *½ cup chopped peanuts** at the end. Bake 18 to 20 minutes, as above.

Variation 2 Sacher Brownies

Make BROWNIES with the following changes: Melt *8 tablespoons (1 stick) butter with 6 ounces chocolate** and *½ cup raspberry preserves.* Omit the sour cream and instant espresso. Fold in *½ cup golden raisins and ½ cup chopped walnuts** at the end. Bake 20 to 25 minutes, as above.

Variation 3 Coconut Brownies

Make BROWNIES with the following changes: Omit the sour cream and instant espresso. Stir in *¼ teaspoon coconut extract* with the vanilla. In a small bowl, stir *½ cup shredded coconut with 1 tablespoon melted butter.* Sprinkle over the batter in the pan just before baking. Bake 18 to 22 minutes, as above.

Tips

* Butter and flour a cake pan to prevent sticking. Lightly grease bottom and sides of pan with softened butter. Sprinkle on 1 tablespoon flour to coat bottom and sides. Invert and tap pan lightly to release any excess flour.

* To melt the butter and chocolate, stir over very low heat in a heavy saucepan, being careful not to scorch the mixture. Or, stir in the top of a double boiler over barely simmering water. To melt in the microwave, place the butter and chocolate in a large glass measure or bowl. (Be sure the container is completely dry; any moisture may cause the chocolate to stiffen. Should this occur, stir in small amounts of vegetable oil until the chocolate is smooth.) Cook on HIGH about 1½ minutes. Stir until smooth. The butter will be hot. If the chocolate is not completely melted, stir occasionally. It will melt in the hot butter.

* To test a cake or brownie for doneness, insert a toothpick into the center. If it comes out dry and clean, the cake is done. If bits of wet batter cling, bake 2 to 3 minutes more. Test again.

* Buy shelled nuts. Chop coarsely on a cutting board with a chef's knife, or chop quickly with a food processor.

24 Chocolate Mousse

This mousse is quite simple to make; there are only 2 steps and no egg whites to beat. It is very, very dense and rich. A little will go a long, long way. I promise. The perfect complement would be fresh strawberries, sliced and arranged on top of each serving, or whole raspberries. Even a slice of fresh orange would be an appropriate little adornment. Or, serve it neat.

12 ounces semisweet chocolate*

2 cups heavy whipping cream

3 tablespoons confectioners' sugar

2 tablespoons orange-flavored liqueur

1 tablespoon instant espresso or coffee powder or granules

SERVES 8 TO 10

1 Melt the chocolate with ⅔ cup of the cream in a double boiler, stirring until smooth, or melt in the microwave.* Cool to room temperature.

2 With an electric mixer, whip the remaining cream,* sugar, liqueur, and espresso powder, until almost stiff. Fold* a small amount of whipped cream into the cooled chocolate. Fold this chocolate mixture back into the remaining cream until smooth.

3 Spoon into 8 or 10 wineglasses, dessert bowls, or coffee cups. Chill at least 1 hour before serving.

Variation **1** *𝒥*ROZEN CHOCOLATE TERRINE   SERVES 12 (OR MORE, IF SLICED CAREFULLY)

Make CHOCOLATE MOUSSE with the following changes: Toast ¾ *cup coarsely chopped walnuts** in a nonstick pan over low heat 3 to 5 minutes. Cool slightly. Line a 9- × -5- × -3-inch loaf pan with plastic wrap. Make CHOCOLATE MOUSSE. Sprinkle half the nuts in the bottom of the loaf pan. Spoon in half the mousse, smoothing the top. Repeat with the remaining nuts and mousse. Cover with plastic. Freeze about 6 hours or overnight, until firm to the touch. Just before serving, unmold on a platter or board. Cut into ½ inch slices with a knife dipped in hot water. Garnish with fresh fruit, if desired, and serve at once.

Variation **2** *W*HITE CHOCOLATE MOUSSE   SERVES 4 OR 5

Make CHOCOLATE MOUSSE with the following changes: Make half the recipe (or make the full recipe to serve 8 to 10). Substitute *quality white chocolate* for the chocolate. Substitute *rum or Cognac* for the liqueur. Omit the instant espresso. Chill 1 hour.

Variation **3** *B*LACK AND TAN PARFAIT   SERVES 8

Make CHOCOLATE MOUSSE with the following changes: Use *6 ounces chocolate and melt with* ⅓ *cup of the cream.* Cool. After the remaining 1⅔ cups cream is flavored and whipped, as above, divide it in half. Place in 2 bowls. Fold the chocolate into 1 bowl. In 8 stemmed glasses, alternate 4 layers, total, of cream and chocolate mixture. Chill 1 hour. Garnish with fresh fruit, if desired.

Tips ** For an explanation of chocolate, see Brownies, Tips (page 54).*

* To melt chocolate, see Brownies, Tips (page 55). Microwave on HIGH *1½ minutes. Stir; microwave on* HIGH *30 seconds more, if necessary. Adjust cooking time for half the quantity of chocolate.*

* To whip cream, see Secrets of a Competent Cook (page 66).

* To fold, see Secrets of a Competent Cook (page 68).

* To chop nuts, see Brownies, Tips (page 55).

25 Simple Egg Custard

Three little words that speak for themselves.

2 cups milk

3 eggs plus 1 yolk, lightly beaten

⅓ cup sugar

1 teaspoon vanilla extract

Pinch of salt

SERVES 4

1 Heat the oven to 325°.

2 In a bowl, whisk all the ingredients until smooth.

3 Arrange four 10-ounce oven-proof custard cups, ramekins, or small baking dishes in a large pan. Pour the custard into the cups. Pour about ½ inch hot water into the pan.*

4 Bake 35 minutes, until a knife inserted halfway between the center and edge of each custard cup comes out clean. Remove from oven and let stand 30 minutes in the pan. The hot water will complete the cooking of the custard.

5 Serve warm, or refrigerate and serve.

Variation 1   CHOCOLATE CUSTARD

Make SIMPLE EGG CUSTARD with the following changes: Into the unbaked custard mixture, whisk *3 ounces semisweet chocolate, melted and cooled; 1 teaspoon instant espresso or coffee powder or granules; and a pinch of ground cinnamon.* Bake as above.

Variation 2   CRÈME CARAMEL (FLAN)

Make SIMPLE EGG CUSTARD with the following changes: Add *another yolk* to unbaked custard mixture. You can caramelize the sugar on top of the stove,* but it is easier to do in a microwave: In the bottom of each of six ½-cup microwave safe and conventional oven-proof containers sprinkle *1 tablespoon sugar and 1 teaspoon water.* Arrange cups in a ring in microwave. Microwave on HIGH 4 minutes, until sugar has dissolved and an amber-colored syrup is formed. It will be very hot. Cool slightly. It will harden. Put cooled cups in a large pan as above. Pour custard into cups; pour hot water around cups. Bake 35 to 40 minutes, testing and cooling custard as above. Refrigerate several hours. Run the blade of a small knife around the edge of each cup. Invert onto 6 small plates. (Or serve in the custard cups.)

Variation 3   BREAD PUDDING

Make SIMPLE EGG CUSTARD with the following changes: Butter a 9-inch square cake pan. In a large bowl, toss *4 cups cubed bread (white, whole wheat, cinnamon raisin, French, or Italian)* with *½ cup golden raisins* and *¼ cup orange-flavored liqueur.* Prepare SIMPLE EGG CUSTARD but do not bake. Heat oven to 325°. Pour custard over bread. Let stand 30 minutes. Pour bread mixture into prepared pan. Sprinkle top with *1 tablespoon sugar tossed with ¼ teaspoon ground cinnamon.* Bake 45 minutes, until golden and a knife inserted into pudding comes out clean. Cut into 9 squares. Serve warm, at room temperature, or cold.

Tips   * When baking a custard, a "bain marie" or water bath is used to slow the cooking. The custard cups are baked in a larger pan which contains about ½ inch hot water.

      * To caramelize sugar on top of the stove, heat the sugar and water in a small heavy saucepan until the water is boiling and the sugar is dissolved. Cook about 6 to 8 minutes, until an amber (light brown) syrup is formed.

MENUS

BRUNCH
Breakfast Scones
Omelet
Broiled Tomato with Rosemary
Apple Dumplings

COCKTAILS
Mexican Salsa (with tortilla chips)
Crostini
Pâté
Educated Shrimp Cocktail with Green Herb Dressing

SOUTHWESTERN DINNER
Tortilla Soup
Beef Fajitas
Tex-Mex Stuffed Tomatoes
Crème Caramel (Flan)

TV DINNERS
Our '21' Burgers
Pasta Salad Primavera
Chocolate Custard

ELEGANT FOR 2
Avgolemono
Dijon Chicken Tarragon
Steamed Fresh Vegetables
Rice Pilaf
White Chocolate Mousse

SUMMER BUFFET

Bruschetta
Salade Niçoise
Cold Rice Salad
Rolled Flank Steak with Salad Dressing
Black and Tan Parfait

DOWN HOME DINNER

Meat Loaf
Mashed Potatoes
Steamed Fresh Vegetables
Brownies

PICNIC

Gazpacho Soup (Thermos)
Cold Roast Chicken
Bread Salad
Coconut Brownies

HOLIDAY DINNER

Stracciatella
Garlic Roast Pork
Mashed Potato Croquettes
Grilled Tomato with Rosemary
Frozen Chocolate Terrine

WEEKEND LUNCH

Pan Bagnat (Niçoise Hero)
Green Salad with
Goat Cheese Dressing
Simple Egg Custard

GAME NIGHT

Skillet Corn Bread
Chili
Apple Crumble

LEFTOVERS

Uh-oh, leftovers. What to do. What to do.

Now, here's cause to rejoice: "Oh boy! Leftovers."

BISCUITS Any leftover biscuits can be halved and toasted (in the oven) until golden. Use as crackers or hors d'oeuvre toasts.

CHICKEN Cold chicken seems nearly as popular as its warmer former self. Can you be found *in* the refrigerator at midnight picking off shreds of white meat? (I can.) However, should you be considerate of others or just blessed with culinary foresight, try one of these:

Shred the meat, white and dark. Toss in a bowl with some of the following: corn kernels, sliced avocado, lime juice, olive oil, a sprinkling of ground cumin, salt, freshly ground black pepper, chopped cilantro, sliced scallions, watercress leaves. Need I say more?

Make open-faced grilled (under the broiler) chicken, sliced red onion, and Jarlsberg or Jack cheese sandwiches on raisin pumpernickel bread.

CORN BREAD (Skillet) Freeze leftover corn bread. Thaw it, cut it into chunks or crumble it, and use for chicken or turkey stuffing instead of stuffing mix. Add sautéed onion, celery, herbs, liquid, etc.

FISH Flake leftover cooked fish. Toss it with chopped fresh dill, a squeeze of lemon, freshly ground black pepper, and 1 or 2 tablespoons of sour cream or plain yogurt for a quick salad. Serve on romaine lettuce.

Flake and toss with bread crumbs (or leftover mashed potatoes), a lightly beaten egg, and chopped onion. Shape into patties and fry in a small amount of oil, until golden.

FLANK STEAK Slice cold steak thin. Sandwich on French bread with arugula or watercress and Goat Cheese Dressing.

GARLIC BREAD Cube, toast until crisp, and sprinkle on salad as croutons.

OMELET Cut any leftover omelet into thin strips. Sprinkle over fried rice or in chicken soup.

PORK LOIN Slice leftover pork ¼ inch thick. Cut each slice into ¼-inch-thick strips. In a large skillet, fry pork strips in a small amount of oil with minced garlic and ginger, until golden. Stir in some cooked rice. Fry, stirring, until heated through. Season with soy sauce. Sprinkle with chopped scallions.

Cut pork loin into strips, as above. For a tropical salad, toss with strips of peeled fresh mango, sliced scallions, and watercress leaves, with orange juice and mustard as a dressing. Sprinkle with toasted walnuts or almonds.

Slice leftover pork ¼ inch thick. Lightly beat an egg with a small amount of Dijon mustard. Coat sliced pork in this mixture and then in plain bread crumbs. Refrigerate 30 minutes. Sauté these Deviled Pork Cutlets in a small amount of oil, until golden.

RICE Use your favorite leftover rice as a filling or stuffing for scooped-out tomatoes or halved green peppers. Sprinkle with a small amount of broth or water, dot with butter, cover with foil, and bake at 350° until the rice is heated through and the vegetable is tender. Serve as a side dish.

SALADS AND SANDWICHES Turn salads into sandwiches and sandwiches into salads. The Pan Bagnat (Niçoise Hero) can be disassembled and tossed *mañana* as a salad.

An Antipasto can be layered on Italian bread as a Genoa salami/provolone sandwich for someone's lunch.

SHRIMP Chop leftover shrimp (if you can find any). Make Béchamel Sauce. Stir in shrimp, chopped fresh dill, and grated lemon rind. Spoon over baked fish, as a shrimp sauce.

TOMATOES (Broiled) Chop any leftovers. Toss into a spaghetti sauce or a minestrone soup.

VEGETABLES (Steamed Fresh) Chop any leftover cooked vegetables. Use as an omelet filling.

In a small skillet, sauté chopped leftover vegetables in butter. Pour on 2 lightly beaten eggs. Cook, stirring, 1 minute. Sprinkle with shredded cheese. Pop under the broiler until puffed and golden. Slide onto a plate for a quick frittata for 1 or 2.

INGREDIENT SUBSTITUTIONS

The following are suggestions for alternatives to ingredients listed in the book. Some substitutes are based on lower calories and sodium, others on taste preference.

BREAD Use a whole wheat or multigrain bread instead of a traditional Italian bread for the GARLIC BREAD, etc. Many Italian bakeries sell a long whole wheat loaf.

BUTTER You may always substitute margarine for butter. Though equal in calories, margarine contains no cholesterol.

CHICKEN CUTLETS There are turkey cutlets or slices available in supermarkets. These are slightly thinner than chicken cutlets and will cook faster. Boneless and skinless chicken thighs are also a good substitute. They may take 1 or 2 minutes longer to cook.

CHOCOLATE Use any semisweet or bittersweet chocolate for these recipes. Milk chocolate will work but will yield a sweeter product. Unsweetened chocolate is not recommended.

COCONUT Many health food stores carry unsweetened shredded coconut. Use it instead of the packaged sweetened variety found in supermarkets.

FLOUR All recipes call for unbleached white flour. If you prefer a coarser, denser, and more nutritious product, substitute whole wheat flour for a quarter or half the flour called for in the recipe.

GROUND BEEF Use ground beef, turkey, chicken, veal, lamb, or pork. Or, use a mixture. If using ground chicken or pork, make sure to cook it completely.

HERBS Several recipes call for fresh herbs, which are not always available year-round. Keep a small pot of chives or a rosemary plant on your windowsill, if possible.

Fresh parsley and dill are always available. Otherwise, substitute ½ teaspoon dried herb for each tablespoon of fresh. Always taste before adding more of the dried herb.

Soak dried tarragon leaves in a small amount of white vinegar to refresh them. Drain and use in the recipe.

MAYONNAISE Use a reduced-calorie mayonnaise, or use plain yogurt.

MILK Use low-fat milk instead of whole milk.

MOZZARELLA CHEESE Use part-skim-milk mozzarella instead of whole-milk. Many cheese shops sell unsalted fresh mozzarella.

ORANGE-FLAVORED LIQUEUR You may wish to substitute a favorite liqueur (raspberry, chocolate, or coffee). Or, if you prefer, use fresh-squeezed orange juice.

RAISINS I have called for golden raisins in some of the recipes. In the Breakfast Scones, dark raisins tend to burn faster. Use your favorite.

There are now dried pitted cherries, dried cranberries, and in some fancy food shops, dried blueberries. Use any or all.

RICE These recipes use white rice. For a brown rice pilaf, substitute brown for white rice. Follow the package instructions. (Generally, 1 cup of brown rice requires 2½ cups of liquid and 45 minutes cooking time.) Brown rice contains more fiber.

SOUR CREAM, HEAVY CREAM Use plain yogurt sweetened with honey instead of the sweetened sour cream (Peach and Berry Shortcake); or use vanilla yogurt. Line a colander or strainer with cheesecloth or a paper towel. Place the colander over a bowl. Spoon in the yogurt. Let stand 1 hour. Some of the yogurt liquid will drain off. What remains is thicker and less watery. Sweetened sour cream is a fine substitute for whipped cream in a shortcake, though certain purists will disagree. It does, however, add a pleasant tang to the dessert and saves you the trouble of whipping cream. Suit yourself. Should you opt for the whipped cream, whip 1 cup heavy whipping cream with 1 or 2 teaspoons sugar and a drop of vanilla. (See Secrets of a Competent Cook, page 66.)

SOY SAUCE Use a reduced-sodium soy sauce.

SECRETS OF A COMPETENT COOK

How did *I* ever make that delicious omelet, pilaf, or béchamel? Why is *your* version always so flat, gooey, or lumpy? It's not magic, it just takes practice. To speed you along, here are a few helpful hints:

APPLE, to core   To core an apple, halve the apple through the stem end. With a melon baller, scoop out the seeded core from each half. Presto.

CAST-IRON SKILLETS, to protect   To "season" a skillet, which will protect the surface and prevent sticking, wash gently in warm soapy water after each use. Dry and rub a small amount of oil over the cooking surface. Heat the oiled pan several minutes over low heat. Wipe out any excess oil.

CHICKEN CUTLETS AND SHRIMP, to cook properly   An odd duo, perhaps, but each cooks in *no* time. Must chicken be dry and shrimp tough? No! Stick to the recommended cooking times in this book.

CREAM, to whip   Buy heavy whipping cream. You can, with a strong arm, whip it by hand with a whisk (or an old-fashioned egg beater). Ideally, use an electric mixer. It does help to chill the bowl and the beaters first. Start on a slow speed, then increase the speed until the cream begins to thicken. When it mounds, stop. Whip the last few "turns" by hand (with a whisk or with one of the beaters). There is one split second when stiff whipped cream turns irreversibly into butter. Don't overbeat it.

DOUGH   When rolling out a piecrust dough, you may find it helpful to flatten the dough and roll it between two sheets of plastic wrap. It is much easier to lift.

Flatten the dough into a circle. Roll from the center of the circle out toward the edge, rotating the circle. (Don't roll from the edge toward the center.)

EGGS, *to separate*   To separate a raw egg (the white from the yolk), crack the egg against the rim of a small bowl, holding the bowl with the other hand. As you crack the egg, the white will begin to ooze. Let it go, into the bowl. Lift off and hold the top half of the shell, keeping the yolk in the bottom half. Tilt the bottom slightly to release more of the white without letting the yolk escape.

Now for the fun part. To release all of the white, gently tilt the bottom shell over the bowl, sliding the yolk gently back and forth into the halved shells. This action should take about seven seconds and cannot easily be described, *n'est-ce pas*?

A small amount of egg white attached to the yolk is not a problem; however, the whites must be pure and yolk-free when beaten.

EGGS, *to hard-cook*   To properly hard-cook an egg, you do not boil it. This causes a dark surface to form around the yolk. Put the egg in a saucepan. Add cold water to come up one inch above the egg. Cover and heat just to a boil. Remove immediately from the heat. Let stand, covered, fifteen minutes. Immerse in cold water. Voilà!

TO FOLD   Some recipes ask you to fold one mixture into another. This is a gentle action performed quickly with a rubber spatula so as not to deflate the volume of the mixture.

Scrape the side of the bowl with the spatula, lifting the mixture onto itself. Give the bowl a quarter turn and repeat until the batter is smooth.

OVEN TEMPERATURE   Buy a quality oven thermometer to test your oven's accuracy periodically.

PARSLEY AND OTHER FRESH HERBS, to chop or to snip?   Many cooks have found it simpler to snip fresh herbs with a pair of good kitchen scissors. (These are scissors kept in the kitchen. Good scissors have strong sharp blades. Some have plastic handles for a more comfortable grip. All should be rust-proof.) Rinse herbs and pat dry. Snip the leaves with the scissors, cutting as fine as you like.

PASTRY   When you "cut in" butter you are breaking up the pieces of butter while rubbing them into the dry ingredients. The end product is a mass of tiny, buttery, floury nodules.

When cutting in butter (for piecrusts or biscuits), work quickly and gently. Leave a few lumps for a flakier end product. After the liquid is added, stir the mixture just enough to moisten the dry ingredients and enable you to gather the dough into a ball. It may crumble slightly. Overmixing makes a tough pastry.

RICE, to cook   Do not disturb. Once your rice is simmering, cover it and keep the heat low. You will hear a faint bubbling. That is sufficient. Don't fiddle with it making nice nice. The rice will do its own thing. After eighteen to twenty minutes of gentle cooking, lift the lid and tilt the pan. There may be a small amount of liquid. Cover and let stand, off the heat, five to ten minutes, to absorb the liquid. Fluff with a fork just before serving.

WHITE SAUCE/BÉCHAMEL, to cook a smooth   This, one of the classic French sauces, deserves a comeback and a place in your repertoire. The key is gentle cooking and more than occasional stirring with a wooden spoon or whisk. If the heat is too high, the sauce will cook unevenly, start sticking to the bottom, and it will lump. Then you will have to whisk like mad to smooth it out. Cook it slowly and gently with light music in the background.

HOW TO CUT UP A WHOLE ROAST CHICKEN

Half the battle seems to be buying, carrying, and cooking the darn thing. When it arrives at table, however, someone is faced with the not-so-terribly-difficult task of cutting up the bird in a less than brutal manner. Here are some tips:

Use a sharp carving knife and fork. Carve one side of the chicken at a time.

REMOVE THE LEG (The leg is the drumstick and thigh.)

Using a carving fork, gently pull the drumstick and thigh away from the body. Cut any skin attached to the body. With scissors, sever the joint connecting the thigh to the body and cut through any skin to release the leg. Place the leg skin side down on a board; cut through the joint with a knife or scissors to separate the drumstick from the thigh.

REMOVE THE WING

Using the carving fork, gently pull the wing away from the body. With scissors or a knife, cut through the first joint (shoulder, not elbow).

REMOVE THE BREAST

From the neck end, cut along one side of the central breastbone through the skin, separating the breast from the carcass. Continue cutting along the contour of the breast. Pull the breast away from the carcass, cutting to release it. Remove the breast in one piece, with the skin attached, if possible. On a three-and-a-half-pound chicken, it is easier to serve the breast whole than to carve it as you would with a larger bird.

REPEAT ALL STEPS FOR THE OTHER SIDE OF THE CHICKEN

For a more attractive presentation at the table, before roasting, tie the ends of the drumsticks together with kitchen twine.

HOW TO STOCK A KITCHEN

The following items are used in this book. Whether you are setting up your first kitchen (or just filling in the holes), this is a guide to the well-stocked kitchen.

The less common items are illustrated.

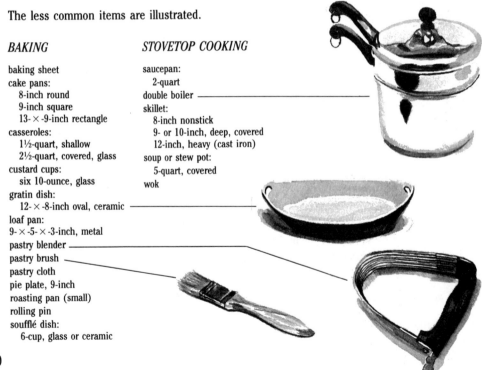

BAKING

baking sheet
cake pans:
    8-inch round
    9-inch square
    13- × -9-inch rectangle
casseroles:
    1½-quart, shallow
    2½-quart, covered, glass
custard cups:
    six 10-ounce, glass
gratin dish:
    12- × -8-inch oval, ceramic
loaf pan:
    9- × -5- × -3-inch, metal
pastry blender
pastry brush
pastry cloth
pie plate, 9-inch
roasting pan (small)
rolling pin
soufflé dish:
    6-cup, glass or ceramic

STOVETOP COOKING

saucepan:
    2-quart
double boiler
skillet:
    8-inch nonstick
    9- or 10-inch, deep, covered
    12-inch, heavy (cast iron)
soup or stew pot:
    5-quart, covered
wok

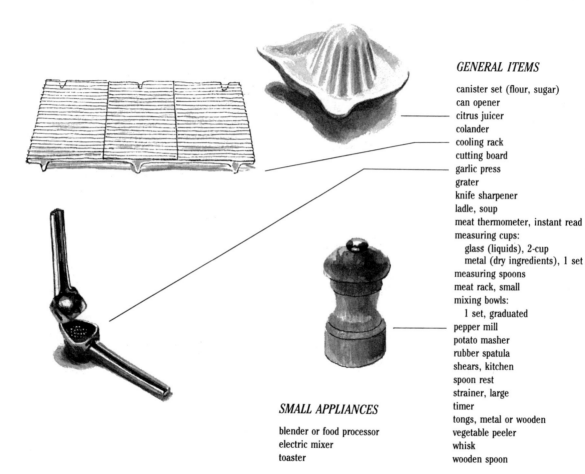

GENERAL ITEMS

canister set (flour, sugar)
can opener
citrus juicer
colander
cooling rack
cutting board
garlic press
grater
knife sharpener
ladle, soup
meat thermometer, instant read
measuring cups:
   glass (liquids), 2-cup
   metal (dry ingredients), 1 set
measuring spoons
meat rack, small
mixing bowls:
   1 set, graduated
pepper mill
potato masher
rubber spatula
shears, kitchen
spoon rest
strainer, large
timer
tongs, metal or wooden
vegetable peeler
whisk
wooden spoon

SMALL APPLIANCES

blender or food processor
electric mixer
toaster

KNIVES

Fine ingredients, fresh produce, and a healthy enthusiasm are all essential to the preparation of a great meal. Similarly, a good set of knives is indispensible.

Well-made knives will last for years. When stocking a kitchen, it is worth buying a good four- or five-piece set. The following knives are recommended for general cooking and for the recipes in this book:

CHEF'S KNIFE

The chef's knife is the most important cutting and chopping tool. A good size is eleven or twelve inches with a six- or seven-inch blade, shaped like a long triangle. It should have a good weight (about eight ounces). The handle should fit comfortably in your hand and the blade should curve up toward the point so a rocking motion can be achieved when chopping.

PARING KNIFE

A small sharp knife for peeling fruits or vegetables, for fine chopping and small jobs.

SERRATED KNIFE

The perfect knife for slicing bread. It cuts through the crust without squashing the loaf.

CARVING KNIFE

A long-bladed sharp slicing knife for carving a roast or a chicken. As part of a carving set, it comes with a two-pronged carving fork.

KNIFE SHARPENER

It is essential that you have a knife sharpener. (A dull knife is a dangerous tool, as it takes more pressure to cut properly.) Look in houseware departments or kitchenware stores for demonstrations. Many restaurant chefs and butchers have their knives sharpened periodically by a professional. Ask for a recommendation. Sharpen your knives at least once a year, more often if they are used constantly.

HOW TO STOCK A PANTRY

It is a rare pleasure to open the cupboard and find everything you need for a particular recipe. Occasionally, in the middle of making cookies, I will reach for the always-on-hand eggs and find there are none. Or there is one...and I need two.

Here is a list of staples to have on hand at all times.

CANISTER ITEMS

all-purpose unbleached white flour
granulated sugar

PANTRY ITEMS

baking powder
bread crumbs, plain
chicken broth, canned
chick-peas, canned
chocolate, semisweet morsels or
    squares
coffee (espresso), instant powder or
    granules, small jar
corn kernels, canned
liqueur, orange-flavored
oil, olive and vegetable
olives, canned, imported
pasta, assorted dry
raisins, golden or dark

peanut butter
rice
sesame seeds
soy sauce
tomato paste, canned or refrigerated
    tube
tomato sauce
tuna fish, canned
vanilla extract
vinegar
Worcestershire sauce

SPICES AND DRIED HERBS

allspice, ground
bay leaf
cayenne pepper
celery salt
chili powder
cinnamon, ground
cumin, ground

curry powder
oregano leaves
garlic powder
paprika
pepper, cracked black
peppercorns, whole black
rosemary leaves
saffron threads
tarragon leaves
thyme leaves

FRESH HERBS

basil
chives
cilantro
dill
parsley
rosemary
tarragon

REFRIGERATOR ITEMS

butter, sweet
capers, optional
Cheddar cheese
eggs, large
mayonnaise
milk
mustard, Dijon
Parmesan cheese, small wedge
sour cream, or
yogurt, plain

REFRIGERATOR—VEGETABLE BIN

apples
carrots
celery
garlic, 1 head
ginger, 1 small piece
lettuce
lemons
onions
parsley
scallions (green onions)

FREEZER

bacon
beef, ground
bread, stale, for crumbs
chicken broth, homemade, in 1-cup
    containers
corn kernels
nuts
turkey, ground

COOL, DARK, AND DRY PLACE

potatoes

INDEX

ABOUT THE AUTHOR

SIDNEY BURSTEIN *is a writer, chef, and food stylist who has worked in New York at Colombe d'Or, Soho Charcuterie, the Box Tree, Bis!, and the Quilted Giraffe.*

He has written, developed recipes or styled for the New York Times, *the* Daily News, Parade, *Time-Life Books,* Woman's Day, Elle, Food & Wine, *and* Chocolatier. *He contributed to* The New Basics Cookbook.

Sidney was also Test Kitchen Director for Good Food *magazine.*

Born in Hartford, Connecticut, he was graduated from New York University. He studied baking with John Clancy and apprenticed at Claridge's in London, England. He lives in New York City.

BOOK MARK

The text of this book was composed in
the typeface ITC Cheltenham Book Condensed
with display typography in Allegro
by V & M Graphics, Inc.,
New York, New York

This book was printed
by Book Press,
Brattleboro, Vermont

ILLUSTRATION BY
CELIA MITCHELL

BOOK DESIGN BY
CAROL MALCOLM